Customer-Driven Strategy

Customer-Driven Strategy

WINNING THROUGH OPERATIONAL EXCELLENCE

by Thomas F. Wallace

omneo

An Imprint of
Oliver Wight Publications, Inc.
85 Allen Martin Drive
Essex Junction, Vermont 05452

Oliver Wight Publications books may be purchased for educational, business, or sales promotional use. For information, please call or write: Special Sales Department, Oliver Wight Publications, Inc., 85 Allen Martin Drive, Essex Junction, VT 05452. Telephone: (800) 343-0625 or (802) 878-8161; FAX: (802) 878-3304.

Library of Congress Catalog Card Number: 92-60661

ISBN: 0-939246-26-0

Printed on acid-free paper.

Manufactured in the United States of America.

10   9   8   7   6   5   4   3   2

To Evelyn

for all the good times—
past, present,
and still to come.

Acknowledgments

I'm indebted to many people for helping make this book a reality.

All of my colleagues within the Oliver Wight group helped to form my thoughts and thus this material; in particular, Don Bedard, Roger Brooks, Jim Burlingame, Doug Burns, Jerry Clement, Tom Gillen, Bruce Harvey, Paul Hemmen, Pete Landry, Andre Martin, George Palmatier, and John Schorr were especially helpful.

Significant outside help came from Bill Barnard of NCR; Steve Barnhart and Jim Stautberg of Kendall-Futuro; Mike Birck and Grace Pastiak of Tellabs; Ron Kowal of Tennant; Frank Merlotti, Jerry Hecker, Bill Miller, and Bill Bennett from Steelcase; Peter Marshall of Formica; Tom Niehaus, Fred Wilking, and Hank Bannon of Dover/OPW; and Jim Sawyer and Charles Cormier of Boeing Canada.

Coco Crum of Niemeyer, Crum and Associates; Bryson Datt of the Business Performance Group; Donna Neusch of Millennium Management Tools; and Bill Sandras of Productivity Centers International also helped a great deal.

From the world of academia, I need to acknowledge the contributions made by Bill Berry, Ron Pannesi, and Ann Maruchek from the University of North Carolina at Chapel Hill; Keith Blois of Templeton College, Oxford University; Bob Hall from Indiana U.; Terry Hill of the London Business School; Jeff Miller from Boston U.; Jinichiro Nakane of Waseda University in Tokyo; and Wick Skinner, Bob Hayes, and Steve Wheelwright from Harvard.

With this book, as with prior efforts of mine, three colleagues played an invaluable role in the critiquing and refining process: Walt Goddard, Darryl Landvater, and Pete Skurla. Thank you once again, gentlemen.

I owe special thanks to Richard C. "Bing" Sherrill for starting me down this path in the early 1980's.

Jim Childs, in his role as editor and publisher, was an absolute delight to work with. I'm looking forward to more of the same.

Last, and most definitely not least, a special mention for the Wallace clan: Evy, Dave, Shelly, Scott, Anne for her fine editing help, and M.C. for an excellent job in her role as researcher. Thanks again, folks, for your support and your patience.

Tom Wallace
Cincinnati, Ohio, and
Bryson City, North Carolina

Contents

Introduction

This book has a very specific audience. It's intended for executives and managers who:

- Run manufacturing companies—as opposed to retail stores, banks, airlines, insurance companies, etc.

- Are concerned about their company's competitiveness.

- Are not satisfied with their company's rate of progress in providing superior customer satisfaction.

- Need a framework to understand how to best utilize today's many technologies and tools: Total Quality, Just-in-Time, Quality Function Deployment, Activity Based Costing, Computer Integrated Manufacturing, Concurrent Engineering, and so forth.

- Have a concern that their company lacks focus—that it's trying to do too many things at once—with a risk that no one project will be done really well, that things won't get much better, and that people will get discouraged and burn out.

This book is intended to help you transform your company into a winner. It shows how to develop a strategic game plan for providing superior customer satisfaction. Here's why it's so important that this happen:

- To be a winner in the 1990s and beyond, a company will need to provide a superior level of customer satisfaction.

- To provide superior customer satisfaction, the company must have a strategic game plan. Leaving it to chance is terribly risky.

- This strategic plan should:
    - Be explicit.
    - Be focused primarily on the customer.
    - Drive specific actions for major improvements throughout the company.
    - Involve General Management, Finance, Human Resources, Manufacturing, Marketing, Product Development, and Sales.
    - Be reviewed and updated frequently.

That's what this book's all about. Its mission is to give executives and managers the tools to develop *and execute* a customer-focused strategic game plan for their business. This will help them routinely make the correct decisions, and thereby provide superior customer satisfaction.

Customer-Driven Strategy

CHAPTER ONE

Is Your Company at Risk?

Is your company in serious danger? It may be. Many companies that thrived during the 1970s and into the 80s have been acquired by more robust competitors . . . or they're limping along with a greatly diminished market share . . . or they went out of business altogether.

Some people dismiss this threat with the notion that we've already felt most of the pain from foreign competition. They're wrong, of course, but even if they were right, the threat to the individual manufacturing firm is greater than ever. Many domestic companies are enormously healthy, rivaling, and in some cases outperforming, the best competitors anywhere in the world.

One can run, but one can't hide. Safe havens or snug little market niches where companies can be assured of surviving and prospering over the long run no longer exist.

CHECKLIST: EXPOSURE TO RISK

Ask yourself the following ten questions, and see how many you answer with a "yes."

1. Is the competition improving at a faster rate than you are? Is it getting tougher to maintain market share and profit margins because of competitors' superior performance?

3

2. Is there a widely held feeling within the company that the customers are unreasonable, that they're a pain in the neck and "they don't understand our problems"?

3. Does the work force—both white collar and blue collar—appear to be part of the problem rather than part of the solution? Is there a strong sense of "us versus them"?

4. Is the company lagging in new product introductions? Do they take too long? Are the new products less successful than they should be, because they sometimes don't quite fit what the customers want?

5. Is it hard to make improvements? Do major improvement initiatives—on cost, quality, productivity, and so forth—seldom generate significant and lasting results?

6. Is on-time delivery a problem? Do your sales people spend much of their selling time making excuses for late deliveries and high back orders?

7. Are the facilities poorly maintained, and is the equipment old and inappropriate for the tasks at hand?

8. Is there a widely held feeling that the suppliers are unresponsive, that they're a pain in the neck and "they don't understand our problems"?

9. Do key people in Marketing, Sales, Product Development, and Manufacturing believe that the product costs are not valid, and thus lead to questionable decisions on pricing, promotions, and new products?

10. Is it hard to get the total organization moving in the same direction? Is there a lack of trust and teamwork between various departments?

If you answered "yes" to some or most of these questions, then your company may be seriously at risk. You stand a good chance of not being around in five or ten years. This is not a shaky prediction; the industrial history of the last quarter-century is replete with companies that fit the above profile—and that were decimated by the competition. U.S. Steel, American Motors, Univac, Porsche, Diamond International, Richardson-Vicks, International Harvester, and any number of companies that make up the American machine tool and lift truck industries, come to mind.

And just because you've survived the last twenty-five years is no guarantee that you'll make it through the next five. Competition is increasing, not decreasing. It's different today from just a few years ago: Today's threats come not only from foreign competition but also from domestic companies, as more and more local firms dramatically improve their ability to manufacture.

In future chapters, we'll look at North American companies that are competing—and winning—against the best the world has to offer; firms from a wide variety of industries, including large ones like Xerox, Hewlett-Packard, and Steelcase, and smaller ones such as Tennant, Tellabs, and Radio Cap. Superb things are happening, right here in North America.

So what's to be done? If too many of the above problems apply to your situation, if you feel your company is in fact at risk, if you want to turn that around and put the competition—not your company—at risk . . . what should you do?

Competing and winning in the marketplace require strategically linking customer and competitor issues into the primary operational elements of the business. The word *operational* is used here in the broadest sense. It encompasses all functions that directly impact on customer satisfaction, i.e., the desirability, price, quality, and delivery of a company's products. "Operational" includes Product Design and Development, Marketing, Sales, Human Resources, Purchasing, Manufacturing, and Distribution.

What's needed is to first develop and then execute a strategy to accomplish the following:

1. *Establish the primacy of the customer.* The customer is number one; spell it out.

2. *Focus all operational aspects of the business on the customer.* Elevating the role of the customer helps to knock down the barriers between departments.

3. *Serve as a filter for decision making.* An explicit strategy facilitates decision making, and increases the odds that the right decisions will be made.

This last point deserves a bit more discussion.

DECISION MAKING—IMPROVING YOUR BATTING AVERAGE

Think about it this way: Of the last ten operational decisions your management team has made, as many as *five might be mistakes* that will come back to haunt you. These mistakes may cause a myriad of problems in the next few years. But *which ones are they*?

Here are several examples of these kinds of operational decisions:

"We're losing business because our lead times are too long. What should we do about it?"

"To which of our four plants should we assign the new product that's being developed?"

"Should we make or buy these components?"

"Should we implement Design for Manufacturability?"

"Do we need to change manufacturing software?"

"The new product won't run on our existing equipment? What should we do, buy new or modify what we have?"

"Marketing is projecting a 30 percent increase in business over the next four years. We're going to need a whole new plant, aren't we?"

"How much automation do we need?"

"We're moving Department 15 into the new plant addition. How should we lay it out?"

"Manufacturing thinks our product line's too broad. Should Marketing reduce it?"

"Should we implement Statistical Process Control?"

"The union's giving us fits. Should we relocate the plant?"

"We're too dependent on outside suppliers. Don't we need to become more vertically integrated?"

"One of our competitors just implemented Gainsharing, and another installed Skill Based Pay. Should we do either one of those? Or both?"

Wouldn't it be great to "mistake-proof" the decision-making process—to know ahead of time that your decisions are the right ones and that they're taking you where you want to go?

Well, within reason, you can. We live in an uncertain world, and that means that no one person or organization will always make the correct decision. But it is possible to raise your batting average on decision making to a very high level. It's also very practical and, as we'll see later in the book, not terribly difficult.

The key is to develop and execute a Customer-Driven Operational Strategy. Such a strategy establishes the following:

- The customer is number one.

- The most important performance measure is customer satisfaction.

- The company's people are the most important factor in achieving customer satisfaction.

- Impediments to providing total customer satisfaction must be systematically eliminated.

- All improvement initiatives, projects, action plans, etc., must satisfy the customer-driven strategy. This is the ultimate "hurdle rate" for decision making.

- All operational departments—Product Design and Development, Marketing, Sales, Manufacturing, etc.—are a team whose job is to deliver customer satisfaction.

STRATEGY IS URGENT

It's essential to create a customer-driven strategy—today. As we rush headlong toward the twenty-first century—with accelerated technological change, fragmenting markets, shorter product life cycles, and customer demands for more customized products delivered in less time—the margin for error becomes less and less. Trial-and-error decision making just won't work any longer.

To win in the near future, companies must have a strategic framework for decision making, one that will enable them to make the right calls virtually all the time. Here's an example.

Excellence in Action:

SIMON ENGINEERING LTD. ACCESS GROUP,
GLOUCESTER, ENGLAND

My colleague Jim Burlingame has worked with Simon Engineering, a very successful U.K.-based manufacturing corporation. Jim has consulted with this organization, sits on the board of directors of several of its divisions, and has served as acting president for one of these units.

He tells me that Simon has a robust strategic planning process, which results in clear strategic directions throughout this multinational conglomerate. Decisions are made largely based on congruence to the strategy. For a decision of any significance, the first test and the acid test is: *Does it fit the strategy?*

John Barker, Managing Director of Simon's Access Group, says that strategy "certainly makes decision making easier." He went on to explain that any opportunity that did not fit the strategy was not worth analysis, and any decision that did fit the strategy was worth study.[1] Further, a project that fits the strategy enhances the value of other initiatives and assets. The operational strategy serves as a type of filter, testing new initiatives for strategic fit.

Not many years ago, Simon was bogged down with unprofitable business units and was the target of a hostile takeover attempt. Today, following restructuring and the implementation of effective strategic planning, Simon has enjoyed significant growth in sales and earnings.

Most operational decisions are not large ones. But because they are so numerous, they add up to a vital difference between competitors.

How do you mistake-proof a process in which people make dozens or hundreds of decisions that together impact the business in very significant ways? Answer: You have a clearly stated and widely understood, Customer-Driven Operational Strategy. With such a strategy, all the major initiatives are tied together. Individual opportunities can then be tested against the strategy. As a result, the number of decisions is reduced dramatically, and much more thought and effort can be applied to the important decisions, the ones that pass the test for strategic fit.

Synergy may also be a factor. For example, you can look at how a proposed operational investment may generate even more benefit out of other existing investments. It may enhance current assets, enabling them to more effectively support the strategy.

These factors—ease of decision making and synergy—come about as a result of the test for strategic fit. And that's made possible by the existence of a strategy. If your number-one competitor runs his business this way, and you don't, you're at a competitive disadvantage. All other things being equal or nearly so, sooner or later your competitor will win.

Here's an example. A capital equipment manufacturer located in the Midwest held a fine reputation in the marketplace, and over the years had done a number of things well. However, they had a fragmented approach to product development and operational improvements. Many of these activities were not mutually supportive. The problem: They lacked a coherent, focused strategy at the operational level of the business.

The primary strategy was largely financial; it dealt with earnings per share, dividend payments, debt-to-equity ratios, and the like. It's fine to have such a strategy spelled out, but *it's not enough*. The customers really don't care about those things. They care about quality, delivery, price, durability, suitability, etc.

As the competitive climate heated up in the 1970s, most of the company's traditional customers stopped buying the company's products. New customers vanished. The downward spiral was terribly painful and difficult.

Though the company survived, today it is about one-fifth its former size, it is no longer a major player in the market, and it is on its third set of owners in less than ten years.

And yet, obviously, the reverse is also true, as is the case with most of Simon Engineering's divisions. If you're the company with the superior strategic planning and execution, focused on the customers—and if your competitors don't do it well—then you'll be the winner. And that's what this book's all about: being a winner. Satisfying the customers. Beating the competition.

BUT WHAT ABOUT THE FINANCIALS?

Some people challenge this intense focus on the customers. "After all," they say, "we've got a business to run. And money is the language of business. Our first priority is the bottom line."

My response: **IF A COMPANY'S FIRST PRIORITY IS THE BOTTOM LINE, THEN ITS BOTTOM LINE PROBABLY WON'T BE AS GOOD AS IT SHOULD BE.** Over the medium to long run, the odds are great that a company focused on the bottom line won't be as profitable as its competitors who are focused on providing ultra-high customer satisfaction.

There is solid data to back up this point, and it comes from the PIMS people. PIMS stands for Profit Impact of Market Strategy. This program has been active for over twenty years and contains an amazingly robust data base covering three thousand business units. It focuses on the impact of various strategic approaches to profitability and growth.

The PIMS data demonstrate conclusively that companies providing superior customer satisfaction[2] generate superior financial results. The numbers show that the top 20 percent of companies in creating customer satisfaction are almost twice as profitable as the bottom 20 percent. The PIMS people list the benefits that accrue to companies that deliver superior customer satisfaction: stronger customer loyalty, more repeat purchases, less vulnerability to price wars, ability to command higher relative price without affecting share, lower marketing costs, and share improvements.[3]

Is it any wonder that such companies are more profitable over the long run? Could it conceivably be otherwise, given those kinds of benefits? Profitability is best attained when it's viewed as a by-product of satisfying the customers. Ditto for low cost; it's best achieved not as an end in itself, but as a by-product of doing many other things very well.

Coming up next, in Chapter 2: the framework for developing and executing a customer-focused operational strategy.

CHAPTER TWO

Strategic Planning—What, Why, Where, and Who

WHAT IS STRATEGY, ANYWAY?

Ask ten people for a definition of strategy and what are you likely to get? Ten different answers. That's because of the confusion surrounding this topic over the past quarter-century. Here are some of the more common "strategy myths":

"Strategy's an ivory tower deal. It's too complex and esoteric."

"Strategy's for the 'big guys,' not for small companies like us."

"Strategic planning is a staff job."

"Strategic planning is counterproductive. Look at the companies that did a lot of it and went belly-up."

"If a strategic plan doesn't go out at least five or ten years into the future, it's no good."

"Strategy's a 'nice-to-do,' but not a necessity. It certainly isn't urgent."

"Strategic planning happens in the executive suite at corporate headquarters. It never filters down to the operating divisions."

13

"Don't waste your time with strategy; it's not necessary. Just go to work on making improvements."

"Strategy is something that should happen every year or two. In our company, we go to a resort for a long 'strategy' weekend."

We'll be debunking these strategy myths, and others, as we go along. At this point, let's take a quick look at another view of strategy, as described in an article in *Strategic Direction* magazine:

"Effective strategic planning:

- is essential.

- is not self-initiating.

- is easy to neglect.

- requires top management ownership.

- must be teamed with Operations Management as integral parts of a single management system.

- must be a line-intensive process, not staff-intensive.

- must be done frequently."[1]

And, as we'll see, the strategic planning approach presented in this book satisfies all of the above criteria. Webster[2] says that strategy is "the art of devising or employing plans . . . toward a goal." And a goal, per the same source, is "the end toward which effort is directed." Peter Drucker says that strategies are the "flight plans that guide the company's businesses."

That sounds fine to me. For now let's not get hung up on time frames, scope, or who does what.

The goal-setting part of strategy (sometimes called the vision and/or the mission) defines what we want to become, where we want to go. For example, when planning an auto trip, we need to determine the destination. (We're in Los Angeles and we want to get to Flagstaff, Arizona. That's our mission, our goal.)

Strategy also lays out the route. (In this case, we have a choice: Take Interstate 15 north to Barstow and then I-40 east past Kingman to Flagstaff, or, alternatively, head east on I-10 to Phoenix and then I-17 north to the destination. We must decide which route to follow.)

Tactical planning and control, which we'll look at in Chapter 8, is also necessary. It's more specific regarding individual actions. It helps us figure out where to refuel, when to check the oil, where to eat, etc. Obviously, we need to do all of these things fairly well—with some degree of competence—in order to get from L.A. to Flagstaff.

A manufacturing company needs to perform far better than "fairly well—with some degree of competence." Driving from Point A to Point B is not hard, because there's no competition—unless you're in a road race, and then it's a whole different matter. Then you'd better be extremely competent. Running a manufacturing enterprise is a race against tough competitors, and the destination is the customers' ongoing business.

Companies need to plan effectively—at *all levels*—in order to consistently outperform the competition. Only then can they achieve their strategic goals, one of which should be to become the best in their marketplace at what's important to the customers.

VARIOUS LEVELS OF STRATEGY

A company's operational strategy is only one piece, albeit a major one, of the overall strategic environment. To get a handle on where operational strategy fits, we need to start at the top of the corporation and work our way down.

Corporate Strategy

Let's take the case of a large corporation, perhaps a conglomerate made up of a number of different businesses. The corporate strategy defines the types of businesses the corporation wants to pursue and why. (Example: Jack Welch of General Electric has established a strategy that says GE doesn't want to be in any business where it's not number one or two.) The corporate strategy also spells out objectives for growth, market share, profitability, and return on investment.

Portfolio analysis—a process used to decide which businesses to nurture, which to harvest, which ones to buy and sell—is often used to help set corporate strategy. Additionally, there is often a strong financial component to the corporate strategy.

Business Unit Strategy

Corporate strategy does not provide a strategic game plan for each division. It really can't do that. The individual divisions are businesses in themselves and each one may be operating in a very different competitive climate. While the corporate strategy may state broad objectives for the business units, each of them should have its own business strategy.[3] See Figure 2-1.

Note: Some corporations are in only one business. There probably aren't many inside the Fortune 100 in that category, but it's not uncommon in medium-sized and smaller companies. In these cases, the corporate strategy and the business unit strategy are one and the same. Instead of the two boxes shown in Figure 2-1, there is only one.

The reverse can also be the case; there may be another level of organization between corporate and the business units. This would

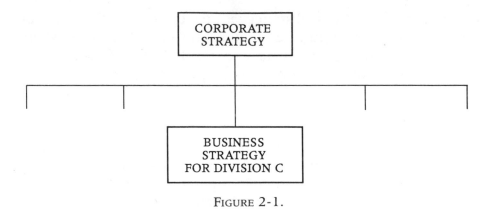

FIGURE 2-1.

be the case where—again, usually in a large corporation—the individual divisions are organized into several groups or sectors. Pfizer, for example, has a pharmaceutical group, a hospital products group, a specialty chemicals group, and so on. Within each group reside the divisions that operate in each business sector.

The overall business unit strategy needs to define:

- The mission of the business unit.

- The future "shape" and "look" of the business.

- The objectives for growth, market share, gross margins, and profitability.

- The markets and market niches in which the business will compete.

- The products and technology needed to attack each market segment.

- How the business will differentiate itself from the competition: wide product offerings, quality, superior delivery performance, price, etc.

See Figure 2-2.

In many large corporations, the financial strategy is most visible as a piece of the corporate strategy, and may be minor to nonexistent at the business unit level.

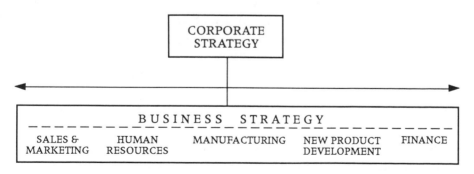

FIGURE 2-2.

Operational Strategy

In the prior chapter we identified the need for strategically linking customer and competitor issues into the primary operational parts of the business—the ones that directly impact on the desirability, price, quality, and delivery of a company's products.

This strategic linking of customer issues into the main operating elements of the business is done via the operational strategy. This is a major subset of the business strategy. For most companies, the operational strategy will cover all, or major portions of, activities known as Product Design and Development, Marketing and Sales, Human Resources, Manufacturing, Purchasing, and Distribution. See Figure 2-3.

BUSINESS STRATEGY

OPERATIONAL STRATEGY				
SALES & MARKETING	HUMAN RESOURCES	MANUFACTURING	NEW PRODUCT DEVELOPMENT	FINANCE

FIGURE 2-3.

The operational strategy does not cover certain aspects of marketing, such as issues of market segmentation and niches, advertising and promotional approaches, media strategies, and so forth. Nor does it cover fundamental research and development issues and long-term technology strategies. The operational strategy does address those activities that impact on the desirability, price, quality, and delivery of the company's products to its customers. For most business units, therefore, this means that a *very high proportion* of the company's people, assets, costs, and opportunities is directly impacted by the operational strategy.

READY-FIRE-AIM

Here are a few words for people whose companies haven't yet done much, or anything, with strategic planning. If your parent corporation has an explicit corporate strategy—one that's helpful to you in directing your actions—that's good. If your division also has an overall business unit strategy, that's great. Your company is well positioned to develop an effective operational strategy.

But what if your organization has no explicit business unit strategy and no functional strategies at all? (This is not uncommon.) Let's say you're the Vice President of Marketing, or Manufacturing, or Product Development. What should you do? You have two choices:

1. Do nothing. Sit back and wait for the rest of the organization to get going on "higher-level" strategic planning, for the corporation and the business unit.

2. In the best tradition of "ready-fire-aim," develop an operational strategy statement, doing the best job you possibly can. Involve your own people and, if possible, your peers on the executive staff and your boss, the general manager.

I urge against doing nothing. To do nothing will result in lost time and opportunities, with the possible degradation of your company's competitive position in the marketplace.

Taking the ready-fire-aim approach will not be as easy nor may the result be as effective as it would if the business unit strategy and others were in place. But developing and articulating your operational strategy, even in a relative vacuum, will generate substantial benefits. It will serve as a framework for decision making, directing actions to become more competitive in the marketplace, so that the organization can grow and prosper.

STRATEGY DRIVES ACTION

Strategy must drive action. Strategy without resulting action is hardly worth the paper it's written on. Here's Bruce Gissing, Executive Vice President of Boeing Commercial Airplane Group, speaking to a group of Boeing managers:

> Now, we can each get a copy of the [strategic] goals. We can paste them on the wall. We can frame them. They will be a nice monument, but they will be GWOP—goals without plans.

We must get the goals into the workplace by setting objectives and defining initiatives to reach those objectives.

Our job is to determine what initiatives to concentrate on during the year. Some are basic, like delivering airplanes. Some are priorities, like simplifying processes.

We can't do all the initiatives all at once. Rather, we must select initiatives that we need to run our business day by day, then add the ones we must put into place as part of our step-by-step process to reach our future vision.[4]

He went on to say:

Our intent is to have the mission, goals, objectives, and initiatives flow down—from divisions, to departments, to sections, to the individual on the shop floor.

That's strategy that works, when it drives actions—on a linked, coherent basis. The result is matched sets of initiatives, employed to best support the strategic game plan of the company.

But it's not easy. One reason is the many fine technologies, tools, and techniques available to help companies improve their ability to provide customer satisfaction. (Most of these are people-based technologies such as Just-in-Time, Total Quality Control, Concurrent Engineering, Manufacturing Resource Planning, and others which we'll be covering. We'll also look at other technologies like Automation, Computer Integrated Manufacturing, and Electronic Data Interchange, but by far the more important tools are people-based, people-focused, and people-centered.)

The richness and variety of today's tools can make it difficult to choose which initiatives to pursue and when. This multiplicity of tools, coupled with the difficulty in understanding exactly what they are and what they do, causes companies to do too many things at the same time. The result is unsatisfactory progress. What's needed is a framework to clarify these complex issues.

THE HEALTHY, ROBUST, COMPETITIVE COMPANY

Organizations are like human beings; they're made up of various organs and pieces and systems. For a human being to function, it's not good enough to have a heart but not blood, a brain but no conscience, muscles and bones but no central nervous system. The healthy person has them all, and in good working order.

And so it is with a company. For a company to be healthy, robust, and competitive, it needs to have all its component parts working well, not just one or a few.

In a company, its PEOPLE are THE HEART of the entire enterprise. They're the core, the center. They keep the company alive. As with a person, how well the heart performs will play the major role in how well the company performs over the long run. See Figure 2-4.

NEW PRODUCTS are the LIFEBLOOD of the company. In most industries, a continuous infusion of new products is as essential as blood to a person. New products revitalize and reinvigorate the company, and enable it to grow stronger and healthier.

CONTINUOUS IMPROVEMENT is the CONSCIENCE. A human being without a conscience is dysfunctional; a company without

THE COMPONENTS OF
OPERATIONAL EXCELLENCE

THE *REASON FOR BEING*: CUSTOMERS

THE *BRAIN*: CUSTOMER-DRIVEN STRATEGY

THE *CONSCIENCE*:
CONTINUOUS IMPROVEMENT

THE *HEART*: PEOPLE

THE *LIFEBLOOD*: NEW PRODUCTS

THE *CENTRAL NERVOUS SYSTEM*:
TACTICAL PLANNING AND CONTROL

THE *MUSCLE AND BONE*:
FACILITIES AND EQUIPMENT, SUPPLIERS

THE *VITAL SIGNS*:
PERFORMANCE MEASUREMENTS

FIGURE 2-4.

continuous improvement will sooner or later be in the same condition. The processes involved in continuous improvement generate a creative discontent with the status quo. This makes it unacceptable for the company to rest on its laurels, and forces it to improve.

The company's FACILITIES AND EQUIPMENT represent a portion of its MUSCLE AND BONE. As with a vigorous person, the healthy, competitive company understands the need to nurture, not neglect, these important elements, and behaves accordingly. The healthy company "takes care of itself" and stays fit and trim.

The SUPPLY CHAIN comprises the other part of the MUSCLE AND BONE. A company's suppliers, subcontractors, carriers, and often its distributors make up an indispensable portion of its total resources. This external infrastructure needs care and nurturing every bit as much as the company's internal resources.

Most human beings have a higher purpose than mere survival. They have a "reason for being" that drives them to do what they do. Religious beliefs, love of one's family, patriotism, a drive to achieve are examples of transcendent goals that have led human beings over the centuries to accomplish amazing things. The company's REASON FOR BEING should be its CUSTOMERS—a passion for its customers' success and well-being. Over the long run, it's hard to be passionate about survival. For most people in the organization, it's hard to be passionate about the bottom line, return on investment, or debt-to-equity ratios. Winning companies establish customer satisfaction as an overarching goal—as their reason for being—and aggressively mobilize around it.

The company's CUSTOMER-DRIVEN STRATEGY serves as its BRAIN. Humans obviously need a brain, and companies need a strategy to direct and focus the activities of all its other elements. Other things being equal, people with higher IQ's will function more effectively. Likewise, companies with a clear sense of their mission, with a vision for the future, and with solid strategic game plans will be far more competitive.

The elements of TACTICAL PLANNING AND CONTROL serve as the company's CENTRAL NERVOUS SYSTEM. These processes transmit signals from the brain throughout the entire organization. They're the "neurological network" that ties together the many and varied components of the healthy, robust company.

PERFORMANCE MEASUREMENTS are the VITAL SIGNS, the company's counterpart of pulse, heartbeat, blood count, brain waves, etc. Healthy people periodically track their vital signs; healthy companies do it continuously.

The human being analogy serves as an important basis for our next step—to look at the conceptual framework for strategic planning at the operational level of the business. It focuses on the nine fundamental business elements we just reviewed: people, new products, continuous improvement, facilities and equipment, suppliers, customers, tactical planning and control, performance measurements, and, of course, the customer-driven strategy itself.

Figure 2-5 shows these primary elements that interact with a company's ability to satisfy its customers, and thus need to be addressed in its operational strategy.

• *Customers* need to be the *primary driver* of your company's operational strategy. Being customer driven, staying very close to

CUSTOMER-DRIVEN OPERATIONAL STRATEGY

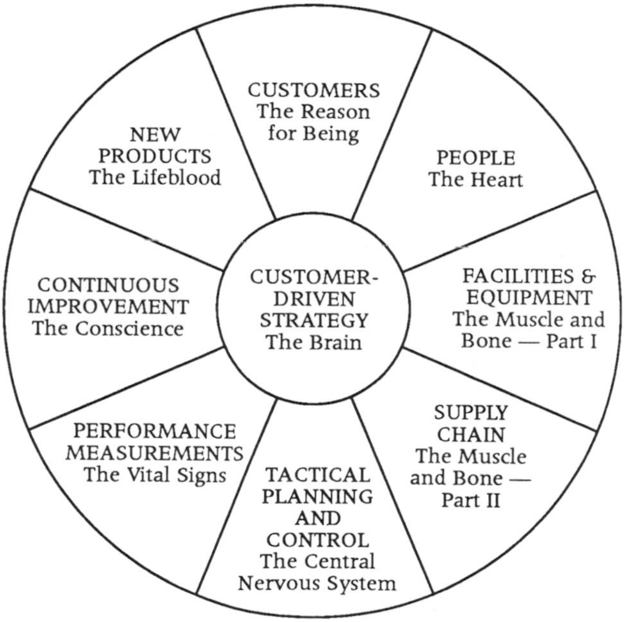

FIGURE 2-5.

the customer, and delivering products and support to meet and exceed customer expectations are what it will take to be a winner in the 1990s and beyond.

Some companies have more than one kind of customer. They have the end consumer, of course, but they must also provide high customer satisfaction to their dealers, distributors, and/or trade retailers. Sometimes the purchase decision is made by someone other than the end consumer, as is the case, for example, with prescription pharmaceuticals, baby clothing, and pet food. Companies need to be winners at serving their customers at all levels in the supply chain.

• *People*. Virtually all companies say the right things about how they treat their people. The winners will be the ones who not only say it, but also do it. They'll be the companies where people not only work hard but enjoy their work; where each person is treated not as a commodity, but with respect and dignity and as part of the team; where people are valued for their minds as well as their hands; where people are empowered to make decisions to improve products and processes; where the company's people are viewed as the most important competitive resource.

• *New Product Development*. Most companies feel about new products the same way that many women feel about men (and vice versa, on occasion): You can't live with 'em and you can't live without 'em. New product development and introduction are expensive, disruptive, time consuming, and essential. It can be very risky. Often, the only thing riskier than launching a new product is *not launching* one. In many industries, technology is moving forward rapidly and product life cycles are shortening. Here the competitive battle may hinge on a company's ability to design superior products—superior from the customers' viewpoint—and to beat its rivals to the marketplace.

• *Continuous Improvement* means just that. It means that every day you can service your customers better than yesterday, and that every tomorrow will find you doing it better than today. That's so easy to say, and so exquisitely difficult to do. It means that the status quo has become the enemy. It means accepting that what made you a hero yesterday may not do so tomorrow. It means that the people within the company will be in a mode of constant change—for the rest of their working lives.

• *Tactical Planning and Control.* We touched on tactical planning earlier and saw that it's not enough to know *where* you want to drive the car (strategic planning). A company must also know *how* to drive it in this competitive race: when to step on the gas, when to slow down, when to change lanes, when to make a pit stop. We call this tactical planning and control; it directs the company's day-to-day, week-to-week, and month-to-month activities in procuring material, converting that material into products, and shipping products to the customers—on time, all the time.

• *Facilities and Equipment.* Here lies much of the "mystery" that the manufacturing part of the business presents to nonmanufacturing executives. It's in the realm of brick and mortar, speeds and feeds, plant layout, automation, etc. Well, I don't feel it needs to be all that mysterious. It's technical, certainly, but so is what happens in R&D, Legal, Accounting, Information Systems, and the Market Research Department.

• *Suppliers.* The supply chain leads in two directions: downward (closer to the basic raw material) and upward (closer to the end consumer). The concept of vertical integration plays a role here. Classically, vertical integration questions were ones of acquisition: Should we buy a major supplier or not? Should we get into the business of making key components or continue buying them? Should we stay with our own sales and distribution network or use third parties? And yet it's possible to get many of the benefits of ownership without actually owning. Supply chain and vertical integration decisions are, by their nature, strategic and therefore must be focused primarily on their competitive consequences.

• *Performance Measurements* come in two flavors: financial and operational (nonfinancial). Most winning companies use a combination of both, with greater emphasis on the operational measures. One reason for this is that most measures of customer satisfaction have a unit of measure other than dollars, and customer satisfaction is what winning's all about.

• Lastly, in the center, is the *Customer-Driven Strategy.* Customer considerations drive the strategy, and the strategy drives all other aspects of the business.

TECHNOLOGIES AND TOOLS

Over the years specific technologies, tools, and techniques have evolved for each of the elements above. Each of these has a name; it has to be called *something*. In short order, that name goes through a process I call verbal shorthand and comes out as a TLA (three-letter acronym). Mix a bunch of TLA's together, sprinkle in a pinch of Japanese, and you wind up with the kind of alphabet soup that can be baffling to many people:

TQC, TQM, EI, EDI, JIT, FMS, AGV, MRP, MRP II, SPC, SBP, DFCA, QFD, ABC, kanban, andon, kaizen, poka-yoke[5] . . .

And on and on and on.

Confusion leads to impatience, and impatience leads to tuning out. Busy executives simply don't have the time or, frequently, the patience to sort out the alphabet soup. And that's a problem, because these technologies and tools are all important. Virtually all companies need to utilize virtually all of them to become and remain competitive.

Another important mission of the book is to help the busy executive sort out the alphabet soup. We'll do that by organizing the technologies and tools within the framework established by the operational strategy model. See Figure 2-6.

Now that we've gone through the operational strategy diagram, let's ask ourselves: Is it enough to be very good at one or several of these elements? Not anymore. You need more than one tool in your toolbox. The issue isn't how good your hammer is. You might have the greatest hammer in the world. But it takes more than one tool to build a house. And today in industry it takes more than one tool to be a winner.

A word about Total Quality. Figure 2-6 references Total Quality Control (TQC) as a technology that supports continuous improvement. Many companies, however, talk about Total Quality *Management* (TQM). Is there a difference?

Well, there certainly can be. Many people use the term TQM to refer to a much broader concept than the tools and techniques

CUSTOMER-DRIVEN OPERATIONAL STRATEGY

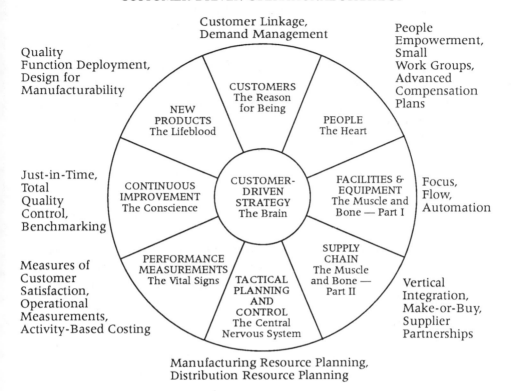

FIGURE 2-6.

contained within Total Quality Control. In fact, some companies use TQM as an umbrella concept under which all of the elements that bear on operational excellence are placed. If you work for one of those companies, you may want to do a mental translation as you read this book; every time you see the phrase "Customer-Driven Operational Strategy," simply read it as "Customer-Driven TQM Strategy."

But be careful, as there's a pitfall here: making "total quality" such a broad concept that it loses its meaning. *The Wall Street Journal*, in a May 14, 1992, article titled "Quality Programs Show Shoddy Results," said: "The 'total quality' movement, one of the biggest fads in corporate management, is floundering . . .

"Despite plenty of talk and much action, many American companies are stumbling in their implementation of quality-improvement efforts . . . A key reason: Many quality-management plans are simply too amorphous to generate better products and services."

Companies who claim their strategy consists of being "a TQM company" or becoming "world class" probably don't really have a strategy. They have some words which may form part of a vision statement, but these alone will probably not be enough to guide their passage through the kind of transformational changes that are necessary.

Winning companies today excel at virtually all of the elements shown in Figure 2-6. Further, because these companies have made continuous improvement a way of life, they'll be even better tomorrow.

Unfortunately, most companies aren't there yet. Further, a company simply can't acquire all the necessary tools at once. It may be possible to implement two or three simultaneously, but you can't get them all at the same time. This means, of course, that some will have to be deferred until later.

But which ones?

A Customer-Driven Operational Strategy is designed to help companies make the right choices. Your decisions will be based primarily on customer satisfaction—which technology, which tool, which approach will help provide the "biggest bang for the buck" to your customers. Here's an example:

Excellence in Action:

BURNS AEROSPACE CORPORATION, WINSTON-SALEM, NORTH CAROLINA

Burns Aerospace makes aircraft seating. Its customer base consists mainly of the major airlines.

Historically, the company has enjoyed a positive customer relationship with several of the large airlines, but not all. Try as it might, it simply couldn't do business with key potential customers. But things changed when Burns developed a highly effective strategy at the operational level of the business.

Mike Beroth, Vice President of Engineering, says: "From the engineering perspective, we designed things to meet our manufacturing strategy. At the same time, we focused our manufacturing strategy in such a way to give us more flexibility at the customer level and the product level. This is a way of life around here now. It is not a minor issue for us, it is a major issue. It has made a big difference to our company.

"We determined that flexibility in manufacturing is a significant issue. It carries over into flexibility in design, which is what we need to meet our customers' needs."

Here's Mike's colleague Doug Kauffman, Vice President of Operations at Burns, speaking about what the company learned as it developed an operating strategy: "Engineering realized that their designs and the materials and processes they were using required a great deal of hard tooling, which means spending lots of money and using lots of lead time to meet the customers' requirements.

"By changing the design to make better use of machined parts and CNC machines, we were able to get the flexibility and the designs we desired. We were able to shorten product development lead time, prototype lead time, and production lead times. It used to take about two years to get a product ready for market. Now we're doing it in a little less than one year."

Here's Mike again, speaking from the design engineering viewpoint: "Product acceptance is my measure. We have developed a completely new product that parallels our manufacturing strategy. Its acceptance has been outstanding, both internally and externally. We have a product that Engineering is excited about, Manufacturing is excited about, and our customers are excited about. It's not often that a new product pleases everyone!"

This company developed a strategy that dramatically enhanced the alignment between product design and manufacturing. It helped them to focus intensely on the customer, and therefore *to do the right things*. One result: Because of the characteristics and appeal of the new product, Burns Aerospace has acquired two new customers. Their names are American Airlines and United Airlines, the two largest airlines in the U.S.

STRATEGIC CHECKUP

- Does the company have a road map, an explicit strategy?

- Does the strategy spell out the core value that the customer is number one?

- Is the strategy in writing, and is it widely communicated throughout the organization, so that the people who are involved in providing customer satisfaction understand where the business is heading?

- Are the most important performance measurements those of customer satisfaction?

- Is strategic planning done at the individual business units, by operating executives and managers?

- Is the strategy tightly linked to the ongoing operation of the business?

- Are operational decisions consistently evaluated for their congruence to the strategy?

- Are major improvement initiatives selected based largely on their potential to provide superior customer satisfaction?

Next we need to discuss operational trade-offs, and why they're bad news. Trade-offs mean giving customers less than the best, less than the best quality, or delivery, or value, or flexibility. Companies that dominate their markets don't live with trade-offs; they eliminate them.

CHAPTER THREE

Breaking the Rules: Zero Trade-Offs

During the 1960s, I worked in manufacturing and materials management for MacGregor Sporting Goods, at the time a division of Brunswick. We shipped thousands of make-to-stock products out of eight field warehouses, and back orders were rampant. I got very wrapped up in "Scientific Inventory Management" and learned about mean absolute deviations, beta factors, and statistically derived safety stocks.

The basic premise was: There is an inherent conflict between high customer delivery service and low inventories. Therefore, you must determine the level of customer service you wish to provide, and from that you can determine the inventory investment required.

I called a meeting. I asked the marketing and sales people to tell me their desired level of customer service, or how many back orders were they willing to tolerate. You can guess what their answer was! Then I asked the controller how much finished inventory was acceptable. She said, "A whole lot less than today."

I said, "We can't give you both. We can't be all things to all people. We can't give you 100 percent on-time deliveries out of low inventories." I started to talk about bell-shaped curves and standard deviations, and to explain the realities of life. They got up and walked out. I could never figure out why they didn't like me.

31

At about the same time, I first heard the phrase "zero defects." There was a large aerospace and defense contractor in my town, and they were heavily promoting a zero-defects program with their employees. My immediate and unequivocal reaction: "Zero defects?! What a lot of [expletive deleted] that is! Everybody knows it's impossible to produce with zero defects. And even if it were possible, it would cost an arm and a leg. Customers would love us, but our costs would go through the roof."

Well, that just about sums up the way it was. It seemed as if there was always a different priority, and we were never giving top management what they wanted at the time.

Of course not. We couldn't give them low cost, high quality, no back orders, and low inventories all at the same time. But they wanted it all, *and they were right*—they should have had it all. But we couldn't do it. So it was a no-win game.

We lived in a world of trade-offs: this or that, up or down, right or left. We can give you X, but we can't give you Y at the same time. It was awful. I can remember thinking: The economists have got nothing on us. People call economics the dismal science. They must have never worked in manufacturing.

It was "us versus them." We were not on good terms with the marketing and sales people. Finance was frightened of what we might do to the inventories. Top management didn't have much confidence in us. Of course, we felt the lack of confidence was totally unfounded. They simply didn't understand our problems.

And that's too bad. Because in a manufacturing company, one of the best things that can happen is for its key players—top management plus others—to have a solid understanding of the elements involved in operational excellence. This kind of company, over time, will become a very tough competitor.

Examples of tough competitors abound right here in North America. Some of them are:

Burns Aerospace

Dover/OPW

Harley-Davidson

Hewlett-Packard

Northern Telecom

PYOSA

Radio Cap

Simon Engineering

Steelcase

Tellabs

Tennant

Xerox

Large and small, privately held and publicly traded, independent corporations and divisions of larger ones, union shops and non-union, businesses based in Canada and Mexico and Europe as well as the United States—these companies are winners, largely because of their ability to provide high customer satisfaction.

COMPETITIVE FACTORS

The issue of customer satisfaction ties right into the question "Why do people buy our products? In the minds of our customers, what makes our products different from our competitors'?" For most companies, it's not a single reason but rather a combination of the following:

On-Time Deliveries: No Back Orders, Shipping on the Promise Date

In most industries, a company's ability to deliver on time virtually all the time can enable it to capture substantial business from its competitors.

Flexibility: High Mix, Short Lead Times, Quick Response

The competitive advantage often goes to the company that can provide its customers with more choices: a broader product line plus products that customers can more closely tailor for their own use, and in quantities that match their specific needs rather than in large lots necessary to qualify them for purchase price breaks. In general, the ability to "turn on a dime"—to respond quickly to shifts in demand, to increase or decrease output rapidly—can capture business from the competition.

Conformance Quality: Conformance to Customer Requirements

This is one dimension of the overall quality challenge. Quality in this context means that the product is doing what it's supposed to do. Therefore, an extremely reliable subcompact automobile has a higher conformance quality than a high-performance luxury car with frequent breakdowns.

Performance Quality: Product Performance and Features

How the car feels when it's driven, the speed at which the computer runs, how good the cookies taste, or the appeal of the perfume's aroma are determined largely by people in Research and Development, Design Engineering, and Marketing. In many markets this is a highly important competitive variable, often at the top of the list.

Price

Few firms compete exclusively on price. Pricing is an issue that should be determined primarily by strategic and marketplace issues. What is the company's overall business strategy, to grow share or to grow margins? The former mitigates for low selling prices, the latter perhaps the opposite. What is the company's position in the market—is it a niche player, competing in a narrow and perhaps upper price segment, or does it compete on a broad front? The former may mitigate for higher selling prices, the latter for a lower price strategy.

In the perfect world, General Management and Marketing should be able to price the products at whatever level will simultaneously attract the most customers and further the attainment of the business goals. However, the world isn't perfect. Often, product *costs* constrain a company's ability to set its *prices* at the best points.

Some companies, typically those in upmarket niches and/or with perceived technological leads, have concluded that product costs aren't a highly important issue. If their costs go up, they raise prices. And the customers pay the higher prices—for a time. Over the long run, a company like this can become terribly vulnerable, regardless of how feature-rich and desirable their products may be. Sooner or later, a competitor will emerge with the capability to produce similar or superior products at a lower cost—and sell them at a substantially lower price. It's no longer good enough to produce high-performance products and not worry about cost.

A look at the high end of the European automobile industry illustrates this point:

Jaguar—sold to Ford

Saab—major piece sold to General Motors

Mercedes—North American volume and market share down

BMW—North American volume and market share down

Volvo—merged with a food company

Audi—hanging on, thanks to Volkswagen

Porsche—U.S. sales in 1986: 30,471; five years later: 4,388

Peugeot—no longer in the North American market

This is not a positive picture. Most of these companies make wonderful cars (although nagging quality problems have been experienced by most of them, including the Germans). However, they aren't price competitive. They're selling their four- and six-cylinder cars against competitors whose sixes and eights offer more performance for thousands of dollars less. The companies that remain in the hypercompetitive North American marketplace are being *forced* upmarket into smaller, higher-priced, lower-volume niches. They are not winning in the marketplace.

Winning companies perceive product cost to be highly important, and potentially critical for survival over the long run. Consistently lowering product costs must be viewed by all companies as a key element of their strategic mission, irrespective of the company's market strategy and pricing policies. Lower manufacturing costs can be important not only in keeping prices low and profit margins high, but they can also help fund R&D investments, support new marketing and sales initiatives, subsidize new equipment, and more.

Winning companies take an unorthodox view of low cost. They don't view it as an end in itself, but rather *as a by-product* of doing other things well. The key is to eliminate waste and increase value—continuously. Low cost will then follow, as night follows day.

We've discussed certain competitive factors: on-time delivery, quality, product performance, flexibility, and lastly price. But this list isn't all-inclusive. Other ways in which companies compete include perceived image in the marketplace (e.g., Rolex, Gucci), unique forms of distribution (Avon, Tupperware), and superior field service (Caterpillar). For most companies, though, the factors we've explored—delivery, flexibility, quality, product performance, and price—are the primary bases on which they compete.

TOWARD ZERO TRADE-OFFS

Let's return to the trade-off issue and engage in some seemingly radical thinking. Imagine being so good at the operational aspects of the business that you have virtually no trade-offs on quality, cost, delivery, and flexibility. Is this a pipe dream, delusions of grandeur, or totally impossible?

Maybe not. Maybe we're already part of the way there. Let's look at some classic trade-offs and see if we can spot a trend in the right direction.

Quality Versus Cost

Today we see companies producing items with defect rates measured in parts per million and, in some cases, per billion. Let's face it: This is *effectively* zero defects. Not literally perhaps, but for all practical purposes it's zero defects. A growing number of companies are doing routinely what many people felt not long ago was impossible.

Why did so many people initially react so negatively to zero defects? Were they deficient in IQ? No, not at all. The problem is that they "grew up" in the world of sampling theory, acceptable quality levels, and a mentality that viewed high quality and low cost as mutually exclusive. As recently as ten years ago, many people still felt that way. Unfortunately, some still do.

The conventional wisdom said things like: "Sure, we could increase quality, but to do so we'll have to tighten up specifications, hire more inspectors, do more rework, reject more incoming batches, et cetera. This will raise our costs. As this happens, we may have to raise our selling prices in order to hold margins. If we're not careful, we'll price ourselves out of our market niche."

Standard thinking in the field of manufacturing strategy said, "There is an inherent conflict between high quality and low cost. You must determine how much quality you can afford, and resource your operations accordingly."

Today people know better. But what happened? What turned their heads around? Well, they've learned from the Japanese, who earlier learned from Americans like Deming and Feigenbaum and Juran, that there is *no inherent trade-off between high quality and low cost.* As quality goes up, costs go down. As an organization gets better and better at doing things right the first time, scrap and rework costs, inspection costs, rejection costs, warranty costs, and other costs go down.

"So what's the big deal?" some of you might be saying. "We know that." Yes, many people know it today. But most people didn't know it just a few years ago, and not knowing it got many companies in big trouble competitively. They got beaten badly on quality and cost and were led into this trap by the conventional wisdom, which identified a trade-off where in fact none existed.

On-Time Deliveries Versus Inventory Investment

Many companies are still grappling with this trade-off, which says that higher customer service levels—fewer back orders and/or late shipments—require more inventory. That's what I tried to explain to my colleagues at the sporting goods company. As we saw, they didn't want to hear it.

At the time I thought they were totally unreasonable. But they were right. The customers should get their orders on time, filled complete, no back orders. A customer order means they want to buy our products, and it's our job to ship the products to them. Finance shouldn't have to go out and borrow big money at prime plus X percent to float a large inventory. Once again the conventional wisdom did us a disservice.

As with traditional quality control, much of the conventional thinking was based on statistics. I sometimes wonder if the bell-shaped curve did more *to us* than it did *for us*. Today, particularly in the quality arena, statistics are being used far more intelligently. They're used as tools, not strategic drivers.

Today, twenty-five years later, it looks very different. More and more, we're learning that there is *no inherent trade-off between high customer delivery performance and low inventory.*

Why is this so? Well, several factors are involved:

1. Reduced lead times

2. Smaller production quantities

3. Better information

Reduced Lead Times

As lead times get shorter, the amount of inventory required becomes less and less. In many cases, safety stocks can be eliminated as the forecast horizon becomes shorter and forecast error is thereby reduced. Ultimately, as lead times become very short, products formerly made to stock can become make-to-order. Then the finished goods inventory goes to zero and delivery performance improves dramatically.

Smaller Production Quantities

As production runs (order quantities, lot sizes) get smaller and smaller, companies can make various products more frequently. Less time between runs of a given item reduces the chances of stock-outs. Inventories drop because less is being put into inventory at any one time.

The key here is setup reduction. Think about the old formula to calculate the Economic Order Quantity (EOQ). Its underlying logic went like this: There is a direct trade-off between the cost of keeping inventory and the cost of acquiring it. It said not to give undue weight to one cost or the other. Rather, balance these costs, make them equal, thereby achieving the lowest overall cost. Calculus was the mathematical tool used to prove that the lowest total cost was at the point of cost equality. Over the last forty years, the amount of printers' ink devoted to publishing articles on EOQ and its variations has been enough to float a Nimitz class aircraft carrier.

Here's a tip of the hat to the Japanese, for their intense focus on setup reduction. Now it's apparent that many people were chasing after the wrong thing with this EOQ business. They were solving for the order quantity when they could have had the answer all along: ONE. The most economical order quantity is one, or a multiple thereof to satisfy the immediate requirements. Perhaps they should have been asking themselves, "How low do we need to drive the setup cost in order to economically make one at a time?"

In actual practice, winning companies don't focus on the formulas. They just keep working to get the changeover times lower and lower—until order quantities can equal one (or a multiple thereof to match what the customers want to buy).

Better Information

I remember a comment from Bill Berry, who's a member of the excellent operations management faculty at the University of North Carolina at Chapel Hill.

We were talking about on-time delivery performance. Bill said that a major factor in the delivery performance equation is to substitute information for inventory. This means it's no longer necessary to "brute force" good customer delivery service via big inventories. Now we can "finesse" good customer service using today's superior tools for demand management and tactical planning and control.

Companies are making great progress tying their customers' production and distribution schedules right into their own, sometimes via computer-to-computer hookups. Ditto for suppliers. Wal-Mart is a prime example of this, "encouraging" their suppliers to establish this kind of linkage. In turn, a number of Wal-Mart's suppliers have the same kind of relationship with companies that supply them.

It's far better to use the customers' information to determine future needs than to use one's own internal data to try and forecast what they'll need. This can eliminate the need to forecast altogether, and when forecasting can be eliminated, so can forecast error. Better, faster, more accurate information—that's the smart way to do it.

To sum up, the trade-off between high delivery performance and low inventories is heading toward extinction—in the same way and for the same reasons as the quality-versus-cost trade-off.

Flexibility Versus Quality, Flexibility Versus Cost

Flexibility means things such as:

- How many different items can you make in a day?

- How many different orders can you make in a day?

- Can you make many small orders and still be efficient?

- How quickly can you adjust capacity up or down?

- How quickly can you bring new products to the marketplace?

Couple very short changeover times with very small order quantities, add in very short production lead times, and factor in very high-quality information and perhaps some advanced manufacturing technology on the plant floor. What do you get? An organization—people and equipment—capable of turning on a dime, being very responsive to demand shifts, providing high mix, and making small as well as large orders—all at an extremely high level of quality and low manufacturing cost.

The worldwide manufacturing community isn't as far along on these trade-offs—flexibility versus quality, flexibility versus cost—as the trade-offs mentioned earlier. However, progress is being made. The day is coming when there will be no significant trade-off on these dimensions.

Given all of the above, **A COMPANY'S OPERATIONAL STRATEGY SHOULD CONTINUALLY DRIVE IT TOWARD ZERO TRADE-OFFS.**

Now, let's not get caught up in semantics. Just as zero defects may not be literally possible, in the strictest sense of the word, so zero trade-offs may not be literally possible. But that's not the point. In the world of quality, zero defects—effectively zero, not literally zero—is happening every day. And that matters a great deal.

Zero trade-offs—effectively, not literally—is attainable. Companies that achieve it will be able to:

- Produce near-zero-defect products at very low manufacturing cost.

- Ship on time all the time with virtually zero inventories.

- Manufacture a wide mix of items and options in a wide range of order sizes without impacting quality or cost.

- Make some of each item each day, as required by customer demand.

- Introduce new products very quickly, very economically, with very high quality.

Sound too good to be true? If you think so, I can't blame you. But today leading-edge companies are doing most or all of these things. Many others will get there shortly. Who are they? Certainly some of them are new to North America: Toyota, Honda, Nissan, Sony, and Mazak, to cite just a few of the more recognizable names. However, some of these companies have been here for a long time:

Xerox, Tennant, Motorola, Hewlett-Packard, and Steelcase, among many others. It's important that the individual manufacturing firm be included in this group, not be looking in from the outside. The winners are inside; it's cold and dark outside.

Zero trade-offs is all about customer satisfaction. And the main thrust of a company's operational strategy needs to be just that: customer satisfaction, leading to competitive success in the marketplace. A strategy that institutionalizes trade-offs, focuses on the status quo, and sets the high bar too low—well, such a strategy simply won't get a company where it must go. For survival and prosperity, your company must be driving toward, approaching, and achieving zero trade-offs.

How long will it take? Unless a company's already well on its way, it can't get there within the next quarter or the next year. But it certainly can start moving in that direction. The next decade? It can be done in half that time, maybe less. And it must be done quickly—or the company might be out of business within ten years.

Here's one firm's experience. At a pivotal point in its history, the company's leaders had a choice: to become a winner or become a loser. They took the right path, and they achieved a level of operational excellence where most of yesterday's trade-offs have been eliminated. And they did it in about five years.

Excellence in Action:

TELLABS INC., LISLE, ILLINOIS[1]

Tellabs makes high-speed telecommunications products, such as digital multiplexers and data switches. The company went through some huge changes during the 1980s, the first of which was the breakup of AT&T.

"The perception was," says Tellabs's president and founder Mike Birck, "that all of a sudden there would be an enormous marketplace that would just suck manufacturers in and create wealth beyond all measure. We certainly know now that didn't happen."

Why not? A major influx of global competition occurred, resulting in five times more competitors, with an attendant shift to more price competition than the market had ever seen before. At that point, Tellabs could have "soldiered on," perhaps making a few changes—fixing this, tweaking that—and run right into oblivion: contraction, acquisition, or bankruptcy.

They went the other way. They embarked on a series of steps that, over about a five-year period, transformed the company into the leading independent supplier in its industry. This achievement stemmed from a recognition by President Mike Birck, R&D Director Ed McDevitt, and others that manufacturing was a—possibly *the*—key factor in the company's long-term survival and growth.

Tellabs had the product, the technical expertise, and the marketing, sales, and service skills. They needed improved conformance quality, delivery, flexibility, and low cost. And, as we saw earlier, that's what operational excellence is all about.

Between the mid- to late-1980s, Tellabs implemented all or major portions of Just-in-Time, Total Quality Control, Manufacturing Resource Planning, People Empowerment, Supplier Partnerships, Skill Based Pay, and Concurrent Engineering. The results: far greater than they would have believed possible at the outset. For the details, see Figure 3-1.

Along the way, what's happened to all the trade-offs? Well, much of the trade-off pain has gone away for Tellabs. Their quality is extremely high; costs have dropped dramatically; on-time delivery performance is near perfect; and many of their lead times are now measured in days, not the weeks that it used to take them. Tellabs is approaching an effective state of zero trade-offs.

Before we move on, however, one last point needs to be made:

Tellabs Inc.
Results of Manufacturing Excellence Initiatives

	Feb 1985	June 1988	March 1992
Monthly production rate	$3 million	$12 million	$14 million
Work force	350	365	265
Throughput time	40+ days	8 days	5 days
Work-in-process inventory	$2.5 million	$.25 million	N/A
Manufacturing space	—	No increase	No increase

FIGURE 3-1.

The people at Tellabs aren't finished improving. They're in a contin-uous improvement mode; they're pursuing new initiatives, new technologies. Their numbers will show more improvement next year, and the year after that, and the one after that. In the winning companies, improvement happens every day, every month, every year. It becomes a way of life.

Until a company becomes highly effective, trade-offs are a *fact* of life. As it starts to get very effective, eliminating trade-offs becomes a *way* of life.

Timing is an important factor. Today you probably can't be all things to all people. It's unlikely that your company can achieve—at the same time—high quality, low cost, high delivery perfor-mance, low inventories, high flexibility, etc. But that's what you need to do. Therefore, it's necessary for the leaders of the company to develop an operational strategy that reflects:

1. The realities of where they are today, that trade-offs do exist and must be explicitly spelled out.

2. The long-term goal of zero trade-offs.

Not surprisingly, it's easier to sell the manufacturing people on the first point and the rest of them on the second. The challenge is to bring all of the key people into consensus regarding today's realities and "tomorrow's" goals.

Strategic Direction magazine, citing a special report in the *Economist*, said:

To survive, manufacturing firms must combine attributes which were previously considered mutually exclusive: low cost, high qual-ity, wide variety, rapid response. Manufacturing goals these days can be summed up in one word, zero: zero inventory, zero delay for the customer, zero defects, zero batch size excess, zero set-up times, zero bureaucracy, zero industrial conflicts with labor. All means must be pressed into the services of continuous improvement leading ever closer to the elusive zero.

FOR ZERO DOLLARS

Some people say, "This notion of zero trade-offs is all fine and dandy, but how can we possibly afford it?" After all, making improvements in manufacturing can be expensive—new production equipment, training and retraining programs for workers, computer hardware and software. These things can cost big bucks. For example, my ex-employer, General Motors, pumped billions of dollars into factory automation—so much money, some observers say, that for the same investment they could have bought all of the Toyota Motor Company.

How can an average company afford these major initiatives? Is it even remotely possible to become excellent, to achieve world-class status, to become Class A^2 in everything?

The answer is a resounding yes! It's not only possible, it's very practical. It's also, in the long run, essential for survival. The question "How can we afford it?" is answered as follows:

1. You don't do it all at once.

2. You do it in steps, in small slices.

3. You concentrate primarily on the people and processes, secondarily on technology and hardware.

4. You generate substantial benefits out of each step: reduced costs, increased sales, and/or lower inventories.

5. You use *a portion* of the savings and cash flow generated out of each step to fund the next.

Do it right and it'll be self-funding. **OPERATIONAL EXCELLENCE IS FREE.** It won't cost you any money. In fact, it'll cost "negative dollars"; along the way you'll free up massive amounts of cash.

Some years ago Phil Crosby, the quality expert, wrote a book called *Quality Is Free*. Phil was right. Now we're taking it a step further: All of operational excellence is free—quality, productivity, delivery, low product cost, and all the rest. To achieve operational excellence, companies can focus on improvement initiatives that are low cost, quick payback, high yield, and proven. Examples abound. Many of them are covered in this book, including:

- Creating high-performance work teams (Chapter 5).

- Creating flow manufacturing (Chapter 9).

- Developing supplier partnerships (Chapter 10).

- Reducing setups and changeovers (Appendix A). (This is not a treatise on how to accomplish setup reduction. Rather, it addresses how reducing changeover time has far wider benefits than just on the plant floor—into Sales and Marketing and many other parts of the business, and all the way to the customer. And it's free.)

As we'll see, these and other opportunities[3] can self-fund a number of initiatives within the company.

Big Bucks

Does a manufacturing company ever need to spend lots of money? Certainly. For lots of reasons—for new technologies, to support new products, for capacity expansion, to replace equipment that's old or obsolete or has been allowed to deteriorate, all those and more. But those should be the exceptions, not the norm.

Make small improvements, continuously. Improve what you have. When you need to spend the big bucks, do so—but keep in mind what Ross Perot said: "Brains and wits will beat capital spending ten times out of ten."

A WORD ABOUT PEOPLE

At this point, some of you may be thinking, "This sounds too easy. Aren't there any constraints to this zero trade-off process?" Unfortunately, there is one, and it's an important factor. It concerns the other fundamental resource, besides money. It's people.

Achieving zero trade-offs consumes no money (excellence is free, remember), but it does consume people's time. And people's time is a finite resource. I'm sure I won't get much argument on that! It's people who are the main constraint to doing it all at once.

The achievement of zero trade-offs is basically a series of do-it-yourself projects. This is because they involve making fundamental improvements in the way the business is run. Improvements mean changes. A company can subcontract a number of things, but changing how the business is run isn't one of them.

Therefore, priorities become very important. The company must use care in selecting which improvement initiatives it pursues, when, and in what sequence. This is where the company's operational strategy plays a most important role. It's the prioritizer.

Here's my colleague Walt Goddard: "Most companies I'm familiar with try to do too much at the same time. They're better at launching major efforts than at completing them. The people become overwhelmed and everyone becomes frustrated. Good strategic planning is critical. It helps to ensure that all improvement efforts are coordinated, pulling to a common mission, coupled with established priorities. Ensuring that each effort has enough of the right people assigned avoids an overloaded master schedule of management expectations."

For example, a company is considering two improvement opportunities: A and B. They both satisfy all of the criteria mentioned above for such initiatives: low cost, quick payback, high yield, and proven. They will both require about the same amount of time by the same people, but there's not enough time to do them both at once. The question, then: Which one best supports the strategy?

Let's say the company's short-term strategy specifies its top priority as improving on-time deliveries. Opportunity A will result in improved delivery performance to a greater extent than B, so it's a "no-brainer" to pick A.

Yes, it's a no-brainer—given *the existence of a formal, explicit operational strategy*. Without one, decisions like this and most others are made in a vacuum. And many things—consistency, focus, clarity, performance, and results—can suffer.

On the other hand, when there is a strategic game plan, then lots of good things can happen. Benjamin B. Tregoe, well known in the strategy field, said it this way: "When you agree on an overall direction, you can be flexible about the means to achieve it."[4]

Another quote, this one anonymous and only partly tongue in cheek: "Strategy, properly communicated, helps to keep the herd moving roughly west." I think that says it well, avoiding the one extreme of people moving off in a hundred different directions, and the other extreme of jackbooted soldiers goose-stepping to their officers' shouted commands.

Let's sum up. Most manufacturing companies have a gold mine in the form of assets and costs tied up in Manufacturing and Operations. Perhaps they were necessary in the past, but not so with today's technologies and tools. This gold mine, pursued intelligently, can provide the funding resources to enable a company to achieve zero trade-offs, and be the *best in its industry at what's important*.

Important to whom? To the *customers*, of course.

STRATEGIC CHECKUP

- Do you know which trade-offs cause the most difficulty in providing customer satisfaction?

- Is there a specific game plan to eliminate these trade-offs, in a sequence that will best serve the customers in the short-to-medium run?

- Is there an implicit belief in the company that low cost isn't important because the products are sold into high-priced market niches?

- Does the company routinely pursue low-cost, quick-payback, high-yield, and proven improvement initiatives?

- Is care taken not to "overload the troops"? Are there dozens of allegedly high-priority projects under way at the same time, each requiring significant amounts of time and mental energy from many people?

From this point on, the book centers around the key elements in the Customer-Driven Operational Strategy diagram. Coming up first, because they're number one: the customers.

CHAPTER FOUR

Customers—The Reason for Being

"Most human beings have a higher purpose than mere survival. They have a 'reason for being' that drives them to do what they do. . . . Winning companies establish customer satisfaction as an overarching goal—as their reason for being. . . ."

Customers are people. Some companies apparently don't believe this because they treat them like a lower life form. But there are fewer of these companies around today and we'll see even fewer of them in the future. They're going out of business, or being forced to downsize sharply—or, happily in some cases, dramatically improving their corporate behavior vis-à-vis their customers.

A list of companies not known for high customer focus would include People's Express and Eastern Airlines; General Motors, Ford, Chrysler, American Motors, and many of their dealers; many discount retailers as well as certain nondiscount retailers such as Sears, and many of the Federated and Allied department stores. There are not a lot of winners in this list.

We could add quite a few hotels to this group. At one point I found myself teaching many of our seminars in Marriott hotels, and discovered that the surface veneer of customer service at most of these places was quite thin. There were lots of smiles but also lots of negative responses, as in "No, we can't do that." Frequently they turned me down when I asked for something different from their standard service, such as a different menu for our luncheon or perhaps a van to get people downtown. I concluded that the company operated to the following set of priorities:

1. The corporate procedure manual.

2. The convenience of the employees.

3. The customers.

I didn't like being number three. I said to myself, "The people who run this company spend too much time reading their ad copy and not enough time seeing how their customers are being treated." I pulled all of my seminars out of that chain years ago and have never gone back. (Apparently not much has changed because in a recent survey, Marriott hotels ranked in the lower half of their price class in overall customer satisfaction.[1])

On the other hand, it's a delight to get really superior service. One gets a sense that the company's people genuinely want to be helpful. Often they say, "Yes, we'd be glad to do that." This makes our lives more pleasant and a bit less harried, and *it makes us want to come back*. Just a few of my own experiences along these lines:

- Dining at the Tour d'Argent in Paris, one of France's finest restaurants.

- Several memorable stays at a small inn in Carmel, California.

- Having my Jeep serviced by one of the best dealer service departments anywhere.

- Buying a Dell computer.

- Shopping at Wal-Mart.

The benefits to these providers of superior customer service? More business. I will return to the Tour d'Argent; I've recommended the place in Carmel to a number of friends; I will buy my next Jeep from the same dealer; I'll look at Dell first for my next PC purchase; and whenever I go to a Wal-Mart, I always spend more than I had planned.

Delivering superior customer satisfaction works. It results in more business. Over the long run, it separates the winners from the losers.

Since customers are people, and "people are us," why is this issue so difficult for so many companies? Companies are managed and staffed by people, all of whom have "hands-on experience" in being customers. It's really quite simple, a variation of the Golden Rule: **COMPANIES SHOULD TREAT THEIR CUSTOMERS AS THEY LIKE TO BE TREATED BY THEIR SUPPLIERS.**

I believe the difficulty in providing superior customer satisfaction is caused by:

- Misplaced priorities.

- A lack of focus.

- Signals from top management that are inconsistent or mixed or simply wrong.

- A lack of the right tools to do the job.

The problem can be corrected by developing—*and executing*—a customer-driven operational strategy.

Saying the words is easy: "The customer is number one," "The customer is always right," "The customer pays our salaries." The hard part is to create an organization that lives by these words.

TRANSFORMATIONAL CHANGE

Transforming an average manufacturing company into a winner involves changing how people view their role. People throughout the company should view themselves through the eyes of their customers.

For example, the people in Manufacturing must reach outside

the four walls of their plant and connect with their customers. They need to meet them, talk with them frequently, and think about what they're told. Only then will they be able to see themselves from their customers' perspective.

This isn't always easy. Let's face it, customers can sometimes be intimidating; they have likes and dislikes, and sometimes they dislike the company's products, policies, etc. Their expectations about quality may be much higher than ours. They're able to point out where we dropped the ball. And it's not always enjoyable to hear these kinds of things.

On the other hand, connecting with customers can be enjoyable—fun in the fullest sense of the word. Manufacturing and other operations people routinely in contact with their customers find it invaluable. They learn how to be better at one of the most important parts of their job: providing greater customer satisfaction than anyone else in their industry.

A corollary to this point is that the people in Sales and Marketing, who have traditionally looked at Manufacturing from outside-in, need to acquire an "inside-in" perspective. They need to look into the plants and start thinking about:

- What current capabilities within Manufacturing can be exploited to win orders in the marketplace?

- Which are the really tough trade-offs? If we could eliminate (or drastically lessen) one trade-off, which one would have the biggest benefits for the customers?

- How can Sales and Marketing help Manufacturing do a better job in providing customer satisfaction?

This also can be difficult. After all, factories can be intimidating; they're often noisy, crowded, confusing. And the people who work there are not always glad to see sales and marketing people.

Over the years, I've talked with thousands of executives and managers of manufacturing companies. Based on this, I estimate that over 75 percent of the Marketing/Manufacturing relationships in the United States are adversarial. Here's an example: Oliver Wight, while teaching one of our seminars some years ago, met a sales vice president from an unfamiliar industry. Ollie asked him: "Who's your competition?" The VP's answer: "Manufacturing."

At the time I thought it was humorous. Now, after the events of the last fifteen years, I've encountered this situation too many times to think the story's funny. It's too familiar and too sad to be humorous.

Changing one's viewpoint won't be easy for either group, and don't make the mistake of assuming that it'll be tougher for "the other guy" than it will be for you. Sometimes manufacturing people have a harder time with this transition than the folks in Sales and Marketing. And vice versa.

Okay, it's tough . . . but it has to be done. Without superior teamwork, what are the chances of consistently providing superior customer satisfaction? Answer: Two chances, slim and none. So the next issue is how do you do it? How do you get Sales, Marketing, Manufacturing, Product Design, and all the other departments to work together as one single team rather than as individual fiefdoms? How do they start to become teammates, not competitors?

A primary element in building this teamwork is to develop a *Customer-Driven* Operational Strategy. The creation of close working relationships with customers must be the centerpiece of the company's operational strategy. This goal needs to be clearly articulated and widely communicated throughout the company, and then the company's leaders must consistently reinforce the message. Live by it. Walk the talk. Make certain it happens.

Remember: Everyone in the company has years of experience in being customers. They can tell good customer service from bad when they're on the receiving end, so none of this will be a foreign concept to them.

But they'll need more than the consistent message; they'll need tools. And today, unlike just a few years ago, there's an array of proven technologies and tools to help people work as a team and provide high customer satisfaction: Quality Function Deployment, Concurrent Engineering, Sales and Operations Planning, Demand Management, and more. (We'll be covering these technologies throughout this book.)

Quality Function Deployment (QFD) merits a specific mention

here, because it's a method of capturing "the voice of the customer" and embedding it into the design of new products. As such, we'll cover it in more detail in the next chapter, which deals with product development. However, the QFD process forces such a strong focus on customer needs that some companies are beginning to see it as a part of their strategy development.

Bill Barnard, a QFD expert formerly with Hewlett-Packard, says, "In my consulting work with Procter & Gamble, Motorola, and the Norand Company, we've experienced the evolution of QFD processes beyond solely issues of product design. My belief is that, due to its intense customer focus and promotion of teaming, QFD will become a recognized tool for strategy setting." I agree. It is likely that the next several years will see the emergence of QFD as a widely accepted component of strategic planning.

Another important approach involves the idea of close ties with customers.

CUSTOMER LINKAGE

Customer linkage—linking a company to its customers—can occur in two ways: physical or informational.

Physical linkage involves brick and mortar; it occurs when a company builds a plant adjacent to or near a customer. This is common practice in some industries, two examples being automobiles and food packaging. Companies that establish physical links with customers are often executing an "incumbency" strategy: They win orders because they're there.

More and more, however, we're seeing that bricks and mortar aren't always necessary for linking with customers on a close partnership basis. Rather, the linkage can be via information. When a company can have visibility into its customers' needs—beyond merely the horizon of the next purchase order—then in most cases it will be able to do a far better job of supplying that customer.

George Palmatier and Joe Shull, two career "marketeers," have written an excellent book on the marketing/manufacturing interface[2]. In it they make this point:

Companies that link successfully with the customers get so close to their customers that their customers' plans become part of their plans. . . .

Customer linking not only helps to improve planning and scheduling for both parties, but it almost always ensures that the supplier gets a larger share of a customer's business. Linking promotes more teamwork between customers and suppliers. The teamwork leads to reduced costs and stronger bonds that are difficult for competitors to overcome, giving the supplier an even more formidable marketing edge.

As you read these words, many of you may be thinking to yourselves: "EDI." Well, maybe yes and maybe no. Electronic Data Interchange (EDI) refers to electronic linkage of one company's computer to another's. Regarding the informational linkage we're talking about here, EDI is often a "nice-to" not a "have-to."

There's a basic principle of implementing information systems that applies whether the system is company-to-customer, company-to-supplier, or internal—that is, within the company. It's called the ABC principle, and it's a variation of Pareto's Law[3]:

The A item is the people.

The B item is the data.

The C item is the computer.

EDI is part of the C item. It involves how the data and information are transmitted; it represents one way of doing that, and the fastest. Alternatives are fax, overnight delivery services à la Federal Express or DHL, and the regular postal service.

Of greater importance than the means of transmission is the *quality* of the information being shared. This is the B item. It does little good to transmit garbage at the speed of light.

Most important of all are the people, the A item, and they're on both ends of the linkage. Do the customer's people understand the absolute need to keep their requirements valid, representing what they really plan to do? Do the supplier's people understand what these schedules mean and what to do with them? Are the necessary people-to-people communication links in place, between the company's people and the customer's people?

Informational customer linkages, done effectively, can provide many of the benefits of physical customer linkages at substantially less investment and cost. "Partnership" relationships can be formed, providing important incumbency advantages to the supplier company. At the same time, the customer company can receive many of the benefits of ownership (of the source of supply) without corresponding investments of money and management attention.[4]

PRODUCT CONFIGURATION—WHERE DO YOU "MEET THE CUSTOMER"?

Flexibility plays a big role in customer satisfaction. One major factor is speed: How quickly can the customers get what they want? Another is giving the customers more choices, more variety, so that they can get exactly what they want.

TRADE-OFF ALERT: The conventional wisdom says the wider the variety, the longer it may take to make what the customer wants. The shorter the lead time, the less chance to provide a custom product.

But maybe this trade-off doesn't have to exist. Much of this issue revolves around where the company and its products "meet the customer." In other words, are you make-to-stock or make-to-order? Do you ship from a finished-goods inventory, or do you produce all or part of the product after receipt of the customer order?

Make-to-stock mitigates for shipping quickly, because the product is already in stock (ideally) when the customer order is received. Make-to-order gives the manufacturer the opportunity to customize and thus increase variety.

Most companies haven't explicitly addressed this issue of "Where do we meet the customer?" Those who have done so have typically reaped some significant benefits, as we'll see in just a moment. It needs to be viewed in two time frames:

1. *Short to Medium Term*: What will the marketplace accept in terms of delivery time? Let's give our customers as much variety as possible within that allowable time.

2. *Medium to Long Term*: Let's reduce our delivery times to become less than what the competition can do, and at the same time maintain—*or increase*—the variety of products we can produce.

That's competitive. What's not competitive is "brute forcing" it via large finished-goods inventories. Nor, in some cases, is it competitive to attempt to narrow down the product line. There's no question that some companies' product lines are bloated, filled with infrequently ordered items from years ago. But that's not always the case. If the customers want it, and the competition offers it, then we'd better think long and hard before we drop it. If the customers want it, and neither we nor the competition offers it, then maybe offering it will give us a unique advantage.

Here's an example of one company's superb results in this area.

Excellence in Action:

DOVER/OPW FUELING COMPONENTS GROUP, CINCINNATI, OHIO

The OPW Division of the Dover Corporation is the country's leading manufacturer of gasoline nozzles. When you pump your gas, chances are more than fifty-fifty that you'll be using an OPW product.

A number of years ago, the nozzle product line consisted of two models. They were make-to-stock products. Manufacturing produced into a finished-goods inventory and filled the orders as they came in from customers. Things were going well.

But then change reared its ugly head in the form of a proliferation of models in the finished-goods inventory. With the onset of unleaded gas, the number of models doubled, to four. It doubled again, to eight, when certain states passed legislation requiring nozzles that recover gasoline vapors. The move to self-service resulted in another doubling of items.

The number of models doubled again and again as the major oil companies embarked on sophisticated merchandising programs that called for the traditionally black plastic scuff guards now to be colored, or multicolored, or with the customers' logos. At that point, there were hundreds of stockkeeping units (SKU's) in the finished-goods nozzle family.

This caused a dramatic increase in back orders, along with a sharp rise in the finished-goods inventory. The on-time delivery situation had gone from very good to okay, and was headed toward poor. The forecasting job had become terribly difficult as overall sales volume fragmented into many more, smaller-volume products.

The solution was to change the nozzle product line from make-to-stock to make-to-order. That's easy to say, difficult to do. But they did it, superbly, via the following steps:

1. Product Engineering redesigned the nozzles, to allow for modularity and ease of assembly.

2. Nozzle production was reorganized into a flow arrangement.

3. In-line test processes and quality-assurance methods were implemented.

4. The union agreed to new work rules, enabling greater flexibility in the assignment of workers.

5. The company's MRP II system was modified to include two-level master scheduling, with modular bills of material.

6. Purchasing implemented supplier scheduling with Just-in-Time deliveries on a number of components.

As a result of these steps, the company is now able to assemble and ship nozzles in less than two days. The customer orders they receive today are for nozzles not yet built, but they'll be shipped tomorrow or the next day.

Fred Wilking, Valves and Fittings General Manager, filled me in on results:

• On-time shipping performance has risen from the 80 percent range to 100 percent—literally. On my last visit to the company, in July of 1991, they had not missed a shipment during *all of that year* and *all of 1990*. A point of reference: They ship hundreds of thousands of nozzles per year, on tens of thousands of customer orders.

- The finished-goods inventory of nozzles is now zero. (Who says superior delivery performance has to require higher inventories?)

- Overall inventory of nozzle components and work-in-process is down 78 percent.

- Product cost has been reduced over 30 percent.

- Productivity, quality, and work force morale have increased. The union is happy.

- The company is more competitive in nozzles than ever. Its competitors are really feeling the heat; some are having trouble staying in business.

- For the first time ever, the company's marketing and merchandising program has centered around the company's ability to provide superb customer service.

One moral of this story: When lead times get short enough, you can make to order, instead of beating harder and harder on Marketing to get the forecasts more accurate.

And another: Dover/OPW is competing and winning through its excellence in integrated operations; they're serving as a key element in the strategic thrust of the business unit. It can—and does—happen here as well as in Japan.

DEMAND MANAGEMENT

No discussion of customer issues would be complete without addressing Demand Management. (This important process is considered a subset of Manufacturing Resource Planning (MRP II), which we'll cover in the chapter on tactical planning.)

Customer demand should drive the company, and Demand

Management is the formal process companies use to ensure that it happens the right way. With this tool, all demands are continuously monitored and managed, to ensure that the demands and the resources to meet them are in sync with one another. It's a key element in being able to ship on time, virtually all the time.

Demand Management has three major elements:

1. *Effective sales forecasting*, necessary in virtually all companies for resource acquisition and for financial planning. Effective sales forecasting will typically involve forecasts in both units and dollars, generated primarily by the people in Sales and Marketing.

2. *Pro-active sales planning*, the details of what Sales and Marketing have committed to sell and how they plan to do it. Involved here can be specific plans by individual, by territory, by product line, and by market channel. The difference between the sales forecast and the sales plan? The forecast represents customer orders we haven't yet got; the sales plan is how we're going to get those orders. Sales planning is pro-active.

3. *Integrated customer order entry and promising*, linked tightly to Manufacturing's master schedule. The key here is linkage. Order entry is not a stand-alone function; rather, it must be an integral part of the company's overall operating system for procurement, production, and delivery. Companies that do this well promise their customer orders for shipment based on information contained within the master schedule.

Please note: Demand Management addresses *all demands*, not only those from "the real customers," i.e., those outside the company. Other important demands can come from sister plants within the same division, other divisions within the corporation, international, testing, requirements for samples, and on and on. Winning companies look upon these people as customers also, even though they're a part of the same organization.

INTERNAL CUSTOMERS

Not only does the total company have customers, so does each element of the work force. These are the internal customers: the

next department, the next work team, the next production unit—
the group or groups within the company that receive "our output."
Examples:

Production is the customer of Purchasing.

Sales is the customer of Production.

*But—Production is the customer of Sales and Marketing for forecasting
and timely customer order processing.*

*Assembly is the customer of Subassembly. Filling is the customer of
Compounding.*

*Production Cell B is the customer of Cell A. The second worker in the cell
is the customer of the first.*

The same principles apply to the inside relationships: close to the
customers via customer partnerships. This means frequent communication, teamwork, trust, mutual respect—and providing superior customer service.

Lastly, if people are good at dealing with their internal customers, then they'll already know how to treat the outsiders—the
external customers with whom they'll come in contact.

STRATEGIC CHECKUP

- Are you speaking the "same language" as your customers? Do
  your measures of customer satisfaction agree with what the
  customers say is important to them?

- What do your customers say about how your company compares to your competition in providing customer satisfaction?

- Is superior customer satisfaction the primary strategic driver at
  the operational level of the business?

- Does top management communicate clearly, consistently, and
  often that customer satisfaction is the company's most important goal?

- Are top management's actions consistent with their communications on customer satisfaction?

- Are customers in routine contact with people from departments other than Sales and Marketing?

- Does the company continuously improve the technologies and tools it uses to provide customer satisfaction?

Coming up next: a closer look at the second most important element in the business, after the customers—the company's own people.

CHAPTER FIVE

People—The Heart

"People are the heart of the entire enterprise. They're the core, the center. They keep the company alive."

One of the best manufacturing corporations anywhere is Steelcase, the office furniture company with headquarters in Grand Rapids, Michigan. I visited with their CEO, Frank Merlotti, shortly before he retired in late 1990. During our meeting, I asked him what's the most important piece of advice he could give to his counterparts in companies that haven't yet achieved Steelcase's level of excellence. Frank's answer: "It's people. The whole thing revolves around people. Sure, they need the tools—the TQC's and JIT's and MRP's and DFM's and many others. But the key element is the people."

Frank went on to point out that Steelcase's people played the central role in the company's becoming number one in the office furniture business, with more than double the market share of its nearest competitor. He indicated that it wouldn't have happened without first-rate, well-compensated, empowered people—over 90 percent of whom operate in high-performance work teams.

Another first-rate corporate leader is Rene McPherson, formerly CEO of the Dana Corporation, who said that if you want to make improvements in manufacturing, you will need to consult with "the world's leading experts." He went on to say that the world's leading experts are the men and women who work in that 20,000 square feet of plant floor space.

On the same topic, here's Grace Pastiak from Tellabs: "These are the same people who go home at night and are deacons of their churches and presidents of their PTA's. They have tremendous problem-solving skills."[1] Yet, as the saying goes, we ask them to check their brains at the door when they show up for work.

Fortune magazine echoes these thoughts: "Cutting labor costs is not the same as maximizing labor's value. The line worker is a great source of ideas for improvements—if he gets the chance to propose them, the power to put them to work, and the confidence that he isn't suggesting himself out of a job."[2]

TRADE-OFF ALERT: The conventional wisdom says that, in order to be the low-cost producer, one must have very low labor costs. Thus, there is a stark conflict between the goal of low cost and the expenses involved in employee pay, benefits, training, and job security. In many winning companies, though, that perceived trade-off has vanished. As we saw earlier, achieving low cost is basically a by-product of doing many other things well, one of which is treating the people well. Let's see how it happens.

In the last chapter, we talked about the importance of people— the A item—in the implementation of information systems. Let's expand that concept, because it applies far more broadly. In achieving operational excellence, in providing superior customer satisfaction, in winning and dominating in the marketplace—people are the A item.

The other elements—such as automation, computer hardware and software, new equipment, brick and mortar, and so forth—are the B and C items. It all comes down to people. Companies that don't believe—deep down inside—that people are the A item, the central element in their drive for excellence, won't get there. They won't make it. Such companies are inhibited by the traditional,

Theory X, command-and-control mind-set which, consciously or subconsciously, acts on beliefs such as:

- People aren't ambitious.

- People aren't very bright.

- People can't be trusted.

For a company whose leaders hold these beliefs, all the words in the world, or the dollars, won't get them where they need to go. Eileen Shapiro, writing in *Industry Week,* alleges that these kinds of underlying assumptions about people led General Motors, under the leadership of Roger B. Smith, to make its massive and largely unsuccessful investment in factory automation. She states: "A lot of that investment went into automation with what seems to be the implicit assumption that workers were so detrimental to the process that what you really wanted to do was replace them."[3]

Obviously, that's not the way they do it at Tellabs, and Steelcase, and Hewlett-Packard, and the other winning companies we talk about in this book. Here's the fundamental point: **WHAT TOP MANAGERS REALLY BELIEVE ABOUT PEOPLE, AND THUS HOW THEY TREAT THEM, WILL LARGELY DETERMINE HOW WELL THE COMPANY WILL FARE IN THE FUTURE.** How a company treats its people will affect how the people treat the customers, and as we saw, this directly impacts profitability and market share.

The good news is that top management has the power to change their beliefs and attitudes. They must learn to trust their people, and to create a climate where it's okay to make a mistake. Trust precedes empowerment, and "freedom to fail" goes hand in hand with trust.

PEOPLE EMPOWERMENT

A hundred years ago, Lord Acton stated: "Power tends to corrupt; absolute power corrupts absolutely." A hundred years later,

Rosabeth Moss Kanter said that powerlessness corrupts and implied that absolute powerlessness corrupts absolutely.[4]

I'll go with Professor Kanter's position. Many of the wrongheaded, counterproductive, downright destructive things that people do are often triggered by feelings of powerlessness, of being totally at the whim of someone else. This affects individuals; it affects families; it affects organizations.

I believe that *empowering* people is what's required to be a survivor and winner in the year 2000; I'm not sure that anything short of that will do the job. Programs for better communication with employees, or enhancements to the compensation plan, or employee involvement initiatives are all fine. But I doubt if alone they will get the job done.

What's needed is to *create an environment that enables the people to make continuous improvements*. Only then will an organization be able to approach the volume of implemented employee improvements coming out of leading-edge companies in North America as well as in Japan and elsewhere. These companies often report twenty or fifty or eighty or more implemented employee improvements per year—per employee. Think of it! Fifty equals one per week from *each person*. The largest number I've heard of comes from a plant owned by a Japanese auto maker: an annual rate of two hundred per employee—almost one per day! This is what people empowerment's all about.

Please keep in mind: We're not talking about "employee suggestion" programs. The word *suggestion* sends the wrong message on at least two counts. First, it implies that the workers aren't sufficiently intelligent, educated, responsible, involved in the business, and/or whatever else to make decisions. Therefore the most they can do is "suggest."

Second, if one party is suggesting, then another party must be deciding yes or no. That other party, typically someone from management, will pass judgment on the merits of the idea. The manager has complete and total veto power.

Of course, that manager is busy; he or she is already putting in more than forty hours per week and really doesn't need one more piece of paper in the in-basket. It's often easier to veto, to say "no" quickly, than take the time to dig into the details.

What might be even easier than vetoing the idea is to do nothing. Just let the piece of paper sit. (In parliamentary terms, this is called a "pocket veto.") Move it from the in-basket to a pending file, then to a permanent file, and finally to a dead file. Or the circular file.

Meanwhile, back on the plant floor, what happens to the people making the suggestions? Sooner or later, after receiving a number of vetoes, pocket or otherwise, they switch off. They've tried to help, but nothing's changed. They know how to do it better (they're the world's leading experts, remember?), but no one seems to care. Management says they're interested in workers' ideas, but their actions sure don't match their words. The employee suggestion program has become an employee rejection program. Back to business as usual.

There's no single thing a company can do to truly empower its people—and that's one of the reasons that so many of these initiatives have come up dry. What's needed, at the outset, is a clear, explicit strategy that's widely communicated. An April 20, 1992, *Industry Week* article titled "The Aimless Empowered," points out: "Effective empowerment . . . does not occur at the expense of structure, direction, priorities, or expectation-setting. Rather, these are the necessary ingredients of managed participation." The foundation for progress with people empowerment is to set the strategy, disseminate it, and make sure the people understand it.

Other elements in the empowerment equation include the array of approaches and tools available to make it happen—small work groups, employment security, advanced compensation plans, and intensive education and training. Companies should employ virtually all of these tools in order to transform their work force into a competitive weapon. Let's look at them one by one.

SMALL WORK GROUPS

One of the hallmarks of winning companies is the use of small work groups—teams of five or ten or a dozen production people with specific missions, responsibilities, and operating guidelines.

Some of you might be thinking: "Here we go again. We already tried that. We had quality circles ten years ago and they never amounted to much at all."

Quality circles ten or fifteen years ago had some serious flaws, one being the lack of decision-making authority. Another was the implicit—and false—assumption that production workers are the primary cause of poor quality. Companies that did empower their original quality circles still have them in place today. (Honda, Toyota, Hitachi Seiki, Toshiba, and other Japanese firms I've visited come to mind; most North American companies didn't do it right.) Empowered work groups are the logical—and effective—extension of quality circles.

In my travels to winning companies in North America, Japan, and Europe, I've visited dozens of plants. Virtually every one is organized into small work groups on the plant floor. Further, in most cases, they make highly effective use of a very low-tech device—the flip chart. During the shift, as team members encounter problems, they record them on the flip chart.

The daily production quota in these plants is to be met exactly. If the quota is 100 units, then the work group is expected to make 100, not 99 or 101. Often, the daily rate is set so that it can be accomplished in less than the full shift. The team then uses the remaining time for a number of things: One might be maintenance, one could be checking their materials and supplies, and—last and perhaps most important—holding the daily group meeting.

The agenda for the daily meeting: the problems recorded on the flip chart. The team is much more than a group of people who make things; it's a team of problem solvers and change agents. Given training in group processes and problem-solving skills, production associates all over this country are showing that they can be self-directed, self-actualized, and capable of making major improvements on the plant floor.

This is occurring in both unionized and non-union plants. According to an article in *Financial World*[5] on companies that are highly successful with people empowerment: "Many are unionized. Many are not. That doesn't seem to matter."

Does successful empowerment happen overnight? Of course not. Toyota's been at it for over thirty years, and my hunch is that as you're reading these words, people in that company are hard at work developing processes to enable their teams to function even better. These people are located not only at Toyota City in Japan but also in Georgetown, Kentucky—just an hour south of Cincinnati, which saw its two General Motors plants close during the 1980s.

My wife and I live in Cincinnati and have a second home in the North Carolina mountains. To get there, we travel south on I-75 through Kentucky. Near Georgetown, just off the highway, a large, modern, attractive plant sits with weeds, but no cars, in its parking lot. A FOR SALE sign is out in front of this empty building, formerly a Clark Equipment lift-truck plant. The plant was closed because "they couldn't compete with the Japanese."

Within seconds another plant, even larger, comes into view in the distance. It's the Toyota facility, employing the *very same kinds of people* who worked at the closed Clark plant or at the failed GM facilities in Cincinnati. Today those people are producing some of the highest-quality cars in the world. So it's not the people; it's how they're led, how their jobs are structured, and what's expected of them.

The transition from a traditional work force into autonomous, high-performance work teams is not quick, nor is it easy. It will take time, effort, blood, sweat, and perhaps a few tears. It'll also take some money, but the investment will be paid back so quickly and so many times over that it really should be a non-issue. And that's the enormously good news here: As you begin an employee empowerment journey, if you do it right, good things start to happen almost at once.

To enable the groups to become as autonomous as possible, some companies establish spending limits for the teams. For example, the team members are empowered to spend up to X dollars for improvements—on their own. Decision making resides within the teams. The people they need to check with are no longer located up the organization chart, i.e., the managers; rather, most of the checking that needs to be done is horizontal—with their customers and their suppliers, internal or otherwise.

Industry Week[6], writing about the Honda operation in Marysville, Ohio, had this to say: "Everybody in the plant is a manager—a decision-maker entrusted with responsibility and authority."

EMPLOYMENT SECURITY

Many of the winning companies—3M, HP, Simon Aerials, Tellabs, Tennant, Thunderbird Boat, Xerox, and a host of others—have a clearly articulated policy along these lines:

NO PERMANENT EMPLOYEE LOSES HIS OR HER JOB DUE TO PRODUCTIVITY IMPROVEMENTS.

Please note: This is not guaranteed employment. It does not say you've got a job for the rest of your life. Nor does it say that you will have the same job that you have now. It does say this: You will not "productivity improve" your way out the door and onto the unemployment line.

Companies do this for the following reasons:

1. Without such an assurance, the people may, consciously or subconsciously, hold back and not give 100 percent—of their minds and hearts, not just their hands.

2. The company's not locked into guaranteed employment. Most of these companies clearly point out that this is not guaranteed employment, that if there's a major downturn in business, they may have to take a layoff. Further, they'll resist the layoff to the best of their ability and, if inevitable, work closely with the people in terms of who wants early retirement, who wants to go back to school, who would like a few months off without pay, etc.

More and more companies are adopting what I call "Painsharing," which simply means that they'll work four and a half days per week, or four days, rather than lay off 10 or 20 percent of the people. It's a lesser amount of pain for everyone rather than a huge amount for just a few people. In some of the winning companies, white-collar workers share the pain also, by getting paid for the same number of days as the production workers. (People who work on the plant floor are often referred to these days as "production associates"—or simply "associates"—as opposed to more traditional terms like hourly worker, direct labor, rank and file. I'll use that term from here on.)

3. These companies recognize, and communicate to the people, that one of the best ways to avoid layoffs is to have sales increases, not decreases. Increased sales often come from manufacturing better than the competition, and better manufacturing comes from an energized, engaged, empowered work force.

4. But what if sales don't increase? What if they stay flat? Since productivity improvements mean that today's level of production can be made with fewer people, the issue is how to get from today's larger work force to a smaller one. The traditional approach would be to lay 'em off. I believe a far better way is to let the work force shrink through attrition.

Let's look at the trade-offs. Layoffs provide immediate payback, right up front. But the bad news is the message this approach sends to the rest of the people; it will inhibit them from making further improvements.

Letting the work force shrink through attrition doesn't mean you don't get the payback. It's merely deferred for a while, while nature takes its course and the work force shrinks. And the good news is that the people remain committed, going after the next improvement.

My belief is that the costs of shrinking the work force gradually will be outweighed many times over by the costs of not having a work force that's 100 percent energized and engaged, one that's fearful for their jobs.

From *Strategic Direction*: "The performance organization of the future will make every effort to secure continued employment, but not necessarily in a specific job or job specialty. Long-term employment requires company commitment to employee development and employee willingness to be flexible in job assignments."[7]

COMPENSATION PLANS

Gainsharing

The term "Gainsharing" refers to compensation plans that have traditionally shared gains in productivity with production associates based on the performance of the entire facility, not just on individuals or departments. In its simplest form, Gainsharing calculates productivity improvements, typically based on a measure of dollars expended versus product produced, and then returns a portion of those gains to the employees.

Gainsharing has been around for a long time. When I was getting my MBA some years ago, they taught me about the Scanlon Plan and the Rucker Plan. These, along with the more recently developed Improshare approach, are all forms of Gainsharing.

What's new is, first, the number of plans in place. Thirty years ago, Gainsharing was about as popular as Total Quality Control (TQC),[8] which means not very. Today the number of installed plans is an order of magnitude greater than thirty years ago. Based on conversations with human-resource professionals, I would estimate that around three out of four Gainsharing plans in the U.S. today have been implemented since 1980. While perhaps not as popular as Total Quality Control, its usage is certainly heading in the right direction.

What's also new is the design and content of Gainsharing plans. Donna Neusch, formerly Vice President of Human Resources at Tellabs, puts this issue in perspective: "Most compensation systems were put in place twenty to forty years ago—and not changed much since. What has changed is many other aspects of the business. Compensation systems are typically not aligned with the business strategy."

Neusch goes on to say that that's changing; more and more we're seeing *customized* plans, specifically designed to support the company's strategic game plan. In today's business environment there are fewer "canned solutions" off the shelf and more customized systems based on rewarding people for improving quality and/or delivery and/or flexibility and/or cost performance—based on which are most important strategically to the business.

Several important things to keep in mind regarding Gainsharing:

1. This is not some kind of "touchy-feely giveaway program" that's being foisted on American industry by "all those liberals who work in Human Resources." Gainsharing is a straight-ahead business proposition. It's designed to motivate people to improve continuously—to "live" continuous improvement—and to work

as a total team. Done correctly, it can yield significant financial benefits both to the firm and to the employees, and I believe that's called win-win.

2. Gainsharing is a "macro" approach; it typically covers all the production associates in the plant. In this regard it stands in sharp contrast to individual incentives (piece rate, for example) and departmental incentives (e.g., more pay for more "earned hours" within the department). The reason: Individual and department incentives can lead to suboptimization; they may motivate people to do things not in the best interest of the total organization. One obvious example is producing more than what's needed in order to get a bigger paycheck. Not only does this build unnecessary inventory, it may use raw materials that another department may need for its production.

Gainsharing is not a panacea, nor is it easy. The Futuro company, a Midwestern manufacturer of a broad line of athletic supporters and elastic braces, started a major Just-in-Time initiative in the late 1980s. This included, among other things, the creation of production cells and the establishment of teams for them.

Traditionally, cut-and-sew manufacturing has been on a piecework incentive basis, and Futuro was no exception. Piecework, however, is individual; it means "every woman for herself," and that simply doesn't fit with high-performance work teams. The solution: Change the pay plan, go to Gainsharing. It took a lot of time and hard work to get the plan designed and implemented, the initial results of which were a 10 percent drop in productivity. This cost the company money. The results today: Productivity is at an all-time high; lead times to customers are dramatically lower; work-in-process inventory is down 90 percent; delivery performance is up; and the production associates and their union representatives are happy.

Gainsharing requires careful study and implementation, so that the right performance is being rewarded. It requires ongoing attention, so that the program doesn't simply become an expected part of the overall compensation package and hence lose its motivational impact. However, when aligned with the strategic game plan, it can be a very powerful tool. In addition to stimulating high productivity, it can add substantial momentum to the continuous improvement processes we'll discuss in the next chapter.

Skill Based Pay (SBP)[9]

This approach says to the production associates: "The more you learn, the more you earn." People are compensated in part based on how many different jobs they're qualified to do. This is quite different from the traditional method, which pays primarily or solely on the specific job a worker's assigned to at the time.

In many companies, Skill Based Pay involves more than the number of jobs a person can do. It also recognizes things like knowledge of Statistical Process Control and other quality techniques, problem-solving skills and other capabilities that make the employee more valuable to the company.

So what's the point, what's the purpose of all this? Here also, it's not a giveaway program. Skill Based Pay, as well as Gainsharing, is a solid business approach to develop a work force that is more flexible, more competent, more motivated, more self-reliant, and more of a competitive weapon. The paybacks can be significant:

1. A more flexible work force lessens the need for queues of work-in-process on the plant floor, and the resulting inventory reduction can be major. In some companies, the annual savings here can outweigh the total costs of the Skill Based Pay program. These costs are not insignificant. Typically they're in three areas: increased payroll costs, increased training costs, and increased administration costs. But the payback—both direct and indirect—can be enormous.

2. A more flexible work force means lead times can shorten and the company can be more responsive to the marketplace.

3. A more flexible work force often results in a smaller work force, as fewer people are required to meet shifts in product mix.

4. A more knowledgeable work force will be better able to solve problems.

5. A more motivated and more competent work force will produce higher-quality products—and as we've seen earlier, higher quality means lower cost.

Back to Gainsharing for just a moment. Gainsharing and Skill Based Pay are not mutually exclusive. They can work together and, where strategically appropriate, they should.

You may be wondering who provides the knowledge and skill transfer in a company using Skill Based Pay. Answer: often the company.

EDUCATION AND TRAINING

Leading-edge companies in North America are becoming places of learning. They recognize that a major part of the empowerment process is to provide their people with the necessary knowledge base. They recognize that the schools don't always get the job done.

Once again, here's a "So what else is new?" You might be thinking that your company has been supporting education and training for years. You pay for job-related outside classes if the worker gets a C or better; you frequently run in-plant training sessions, you encourage membership in professional organizations such as ASQC, SME, APICS, AMA, and others.

Great. Keep doing it. You're well on the way to where you need to be. You might also want to:

1. Put even more emphasis on the availability of these opportunities.

2. Provide more in-company generic education, as opposed to specific training, on fundamentals like basic mathematics (to support the learning of statistics, which supports the learning of Statistical Process Control, which supports higher-quality products at lower cost) and fundamental literacy tools such as reading, spelling, and grammar. For a lot of companies, many of their employees have as their first language something other than English; further, many of the English speakers have not been supplied with adequate skills due to the sorry

state of some of the public-school systems in the U.S. More on this in a minute.

3. Expand your in-company training, and focus it on objectives that support the strategic game plan. This is important because existing education and training programs within companies often have vague, unfocused objectives. As such it can be difficult to see where you get your "bang for the buck." And because of that, those programs are often one of the first things to get cut when times get tough.

The company's education and training process should have as its objectives things such as: creating a highly competent and empowered work force, enhancing problem-solving abilities, and equipping people with the communications skills necessary for close customer contact and group interaction.

Excellence in Action:

MILLIKEN AND COMPANY, SPARTANBURG, SOUTH CAROLINA[10]

One of the most productive work forces in the U.S. is at Milliken, the textile manufacturer. Milliken wraps its approach to people around the "Four E's"—educate, equip, entrust, empower. Let's focus on the first one.

It seems that the South Carolina public-school system isn't exactly a paragon of educational excellence; it ranks near the bottom among all fifty states.

Newly hired production associates at Milliken hold, on average, eighth-grade educational equivalency, so the company offers workers literacy and other basic education at the end of the work shift. They feel this is important, serving as a foundation for the more specific training that will follow.

Training at Milliken is not only O-J-T (on-the-job training), but the company provides each associate twenty or more hours of job-related classroom training per year. This involves topics such as quality processes, teamwork, problem solving, housekeeping—with a good dose of cross-training added to enhance work force flexibility.

Like all winning companies, Milliken stays close to the customer. Its surveys indicate that some of the primary deterrents to customer satisfaction in its business are poor quality, late deliveries, long lead times, and an indifferent attitude on the part of the people who deal with customers. Indifference ranks highest in the problem hierarchy.

Customer Partnership Teams, staffed heavily with production associates, "now work with customers, cutting across organizational boundaries to solve problems and uncover opportunities. The guidelines for these teams sound as if they were straight from Tom Peters: Spend time with customers. Listen and *understand*. Focus on needs. Keep every promise. Respond quickly to concerns. . . ."

Well, I suspect you'll agree that production associates and others need skills to do these kinds of things. And people aren't born with these skills; they're the result of education and training. Furthermore, the education and training for many of these skills do not take place in the local high schools. No, it takes place within the four walls of Milliken.

"Ten years ago, autocratic management was the norm at Milliken. Plants ran full tilt, seven days a week, three shifts a day. The textile business was a tough business. Managers went for the marginal dollar and argued for longer lead times, catering to large orders and neglecting small ones. Only the large customers commanded attention from the Sales Department. Relationships were adversarial with customers, workers, and suppliers. If a plant threatened to unionize, it was closed. Suppliers received similar treatment."

Today it's not the same company it was then. It looks different and it *is* different. Here's why:

No time clocks.

No reserved parking places.

No private offices.

First-name relationships.

A flatter, "de-layered" organization.

Close customer contacts.

Enormous amounts of recognition for good things done.

Results: major gains in customer satisfaction, quality, productivity, morale.

- Example: In a recent year, the company implemented over 2,500 process improvements.

- Example: The textile industry is low-pay and high turnover; worker attendance has traditionally been a major problem. At Milliken it runs above 99 percent.

- Example: In 1989, Milliken won the Malcolm Baldrige National Quality Award. (The Baldrige Award is discussed in Chapter 7.)

- Example: *They are not resting on their laurels.* They continue to work hard in order to get better and better.

My associate Darryl Landvater, who's consulted with Milliken, says, "Milliken utilizes their human resources extremely well. Many companies with highly talented people aren't fully effective in getting all that talent to produce results. Milliken people get 'more horsepower to the road' than any other company I've ever seen, and I've seen hundreds of them over the years." That's a good analogy. The issue is not how much power you have under the hood; it's how much you can put on the pavement.

HIRING PRACTICES

If a company's going to invest a lot of dollars in its people, encourage and empower them to make decisions, and trust them to do the right things, doesn't it stand to reason that the company should take a good deal of care when it hires the people in the first place?

Certainly it does, and this is exactly the way that most of the winning companies do it. They invest substantial amounts of time in people before they're ever hired—in interviewing (by a wide variety of people, possibly including production associates from the team with the opening), in testing for job-related skills, and in evaluating various candidates. Further, most of those people don't make the cut; the company doesn't hire them. Sounds like the company may be wasting a lot of time on people they're not going to hire.

Quite the contrary. Winning companies don't begrudge this extra effort, because when they do hire someone, they're almost certain they've got "a keeper." That's a term I've heard used in conjunction with the National Football League draft. And when you think about it, a winning football team is a good analogy for what we're talking about here. Winning football teams don't simply "draft" the next player to show up, and winning companies don't either.

MIDDLE MANAGEMENT AND FIRST-LINE SUPERVISION

Throughout this chapter we've been focusing on people who work on the plant floor, the people whom Rene McPherson called the world's leading experts. In your company, the world's leading experts aren't confined to the plant floor as equipment operators.

Some of your other world's leading experts work on the plant floor, but in a supervisory role. And as a company moves to an empowered work force with small, high-performance teams, the role of the first-line supervisor is critical. And the change can be very difficult. Donna Neusch: "Often management assumes that the supervisors are with the program. But they're not; they're on the sidelines, watching 'their jobs being whittled away.' Too often management has simply assumed they'll adapt, and hasn't provided adequate training and support."

This transition requires supervisors to dramatically modify their behavior and change the way they do their jobs by about 180 degrees. The role of the supervisor changes from:

- Boss to coach.
- Enforcer to facilitator.
- Disciplinarian to adviser.
- Loner to team member.

Many of your world's leading experts are production associates. Others are in Purchasing, Sales, Production Control, Product Design, Marketing, Finance, etc. Some of them are supervisors; some are specialists; others are managers.

The 1980s have not been kind to middle management. Their ranks have contracted, dramatically in some cases, as companies have "de-layered." Many middle managers are being asked to do more than ever before, often with the same resources and tools.

Please consider this: As you empower the work force on the plant floor, do the same for your first-line supervisors and middle managers. In many companies, they're hamstrung by excessive rules, regulations, and procedures; often their true decision-making capabilities are sharply constrained. This makes their jobs more difficult, more frustrating, and much less fun.

If that's the way it is where you work, change it. Trust your managers and supervisors. Teach them. Empower them. Help them to become leaders.

Here's Dr. Donald McAdams of the American Productivity and Quality Center in Houston: "We are living in a tremendous information revolution, equal to that of the industrial or agricultural revolutions. And the kind of work that is required by the information revolution is best done by teams. And teams work because they conform to social needs. We are social animals, and we like working together. By helping to structure that natural instinct, work teams will create more enjoyable work environments and more profitable businesses."

STRATEGIC CHECKUP

- Do the company's actions regarding its people match its words about how important they are?

- Is the company's focus on maximizing its people's value, not minimizing their cost?

- Does the company truly *trust* its people? (Trust is a prerequisite for empowerment.)

- Do the people have the assurance that they will not "productivity improve" themselves out of a job?

- Are the company's compensation and training processes aligned with its strategic direction?

- Does the company make serious efforts to hire better people than the competition? Do the compensation and benefit policies support this?

Next: the good news about new products.

CHAPTER SIX

New Products—
The Lifeblood

"A continuous infusion of new products is essential. . . .
New products revitalize and reinvigorate the company,
and enable it to grow stronger and healthier."

Military fighter pilots have a saying about aerial combat:
"He who sees first wins." Chances are, the guy who "sees" the
enemy, visually or electronically, before the enemy sees him will
win the dogfight.

Is this always the case? No, other factors can play a part in
neutralizing an early advantage: pilot skill, aircraft and weapons
capabilities, fuel status, lady luck. But the saying is true often
enough to make it a set of words to live by. Literally.

CRITICAL ISSUES FOR NEW PRODUCT DEVELOPMENT

Let's modify that axiom to fit the world of industrial combat, as
regards introducing new products: "He who launches first wins."
The company that's first to the marketplace with the new product
enjoys a significant advantage over its rivals. Sure, it can fritter

away the early advantage via an inferior design, poor quality, lack of product to ship, and lots of other problems.

Time to market, then, that being the elapsed time between the start of development and shipping the product, is an extremely important competitive variable. Let's capture that, in Figure 6-1.

CRITICAL ISSUES FOR NEW PRODUCT DEVELOPMENT
1.
2. Time to market
3.

FIGURE 6-1.

Time to market's very important, but it's not the only thing that needs to be done well. Think back several decades to the early Japanese efforts to sell automobiles in North America. The early Toyotas and Hondas and Suburus were introduced on a timely basis, but they were simply terrible cars. They failed.

So getting to the market first isn't the only issue. Other ways to mess up a timely new product launch include:

• Bad quality.

• Bad delivery.

• A selling price that's too high.

• All of the above.

The NEC Ultralite notebook computer comes to mind. The design was great: a 4.4-lb. DOS-based personal computer. Quality was fine. The problem? They couldn't ship. Massive back orders went unfilled for, in some cases, up to a year. In the meantime, the competition was able to enter the market effectively, and NEC lost significant market position.

In Japan, North America, and elsewhere, people have lost sight of the fact that it's not enough to get a product designed. People have to make it and ship it—at a cost that allows a competitive price, with high quality, on time. So let's capture this, in Figure 6-2.

CRITICAL ISSUES FOR NEW PRODUCT DEVELOPMENT
1.
2. Time to market
3. Price, quality, and delivery

FIGURE 6-2.

The last strategic consideration we'll mention is perhaps more subtle than the other two. However, it's at least as important as the other two, and if there is such a thing as first among equals, this may be it. It has to do with the customers, the people who will buy and then use the product.

One more time, let's think about losing the advantage from a first-to-market product launch. Isn't it possible to launch the new product quickly, at or above the required conformance quality, ship it on time, at a competitive price—and still have a failure?

Sure, it's possible. This happens when the customers don't like the product. It is not pleasing to them. It "looks good on paper," but in actual practice it doesn't feel good, or it's hard to use, or it doesn't do everything it should as well as it should, or it's annoying, or whatever. A common symptom of this: when initial sales of the new product are good, but repeat business drops off sharply. New Coke is a classic example here (no pun intended). Everything about the product launch went wonderfully . . . except the customers didn't like it.

When a new product launch fails, the company may have done almost everything right—everything except the most important thing, which is to listen, intently, to the voice of the customer. To "get inside of their heads." To determine what they're saying, and what they're not saying that's important. See Figure 6-3.

CRITICAL ISSUES FOR NEW PRODUCT DEVELOPMENT
1. Voice of customer
2. Time to market
3. Price, quality, and delivery

FIGURE 6-3.

Saying it in different words, winning companies develop the right product (right in all respects, some of which may be quite subtle), bring it to market quickly, and execute the launch well.

There's lots of good news here. There are tools to support each one of these critical issues—proven, effective tools that North American companies are using to win in the marketplace, companies such as Hewlett-Packard, NCR, Motorola, Beckman Instruments, to name just a few. For an overview of these tools and where they fit, take a look at Figure 6-4.

CRITICAL ISSUES FOR NEW PRODUCT DEVELOPMENT	SUPPORTING TOOLS
1. Voice of the customer	Quality Function Deployment (QDP)
2. Time-to-market	Design for Manufacturability (DFM)
3. Price, quality, and delivery	Both of the above

FIGURE 6-4.

The concepts in Figure 6-4 are generalizations. There is overlap in how the tools affect the critical issues. Quality Function Deployment will help shorten time-to-market; Design for Manufacturability certainly helps in getting the voice of the customer into the product design. But each of these tools impacts more heavily in the areas indicated. (Just-in-Time, Total Quality Control, and Manufacturing Resource Planning also play a significant role here.)

The terminology can get a bit tricky here. Other terms used in this part of the industrial world include Concurrent Engineering, Simultaneous Engineering, Design for Assembly, Design for Manufacturability and Assembly, Design/Build, Parallel Release, and Design for Competitive Advantage (just some of the ones that I've come across). For purposes of simplicity and clarity, I've included these under the concept of Design for Manufacturability; they are treated as subsets of DFM. More on this later, but for now let's take a look at . . .

QUALITY FUNCTION DEPLOYMENT (QFD)

As we saw earlier, QFD is a tool to get the voice of the customer deeply embedded in the product. It's also misnamed. You see, QFD is not primarily a quality tool—in the narrow sense of the word—although it has enormous impact on quality as perceived by the customer. Its primary impact is on product features and performance—in other words, performance quality as opposed to conformance-to-requirements quality. QFD's mission is to rigorously define a product's requirements and embed those requirements into the design of the product.

The term Quality Function Deployment is derived from a Japanese phrase which didn't translate very well. The English word *quality* has several meanings, one of which is "attribute" or "characteristic" (as in "Atilla the Hun had many unfortunate qualities"). When I hear the term Quality Function Deployment, I mentally translate quality function into product characteristics and deployment into development. For me, QFD comes out as the Development of Product Characteristics.

Whatever it's called, QFD is a rigorous, structured methodology that:

- Captures customer needs, concerns, and desires, and breaks them down into finer and more focused elements. (What do the customers really want?)

- Translates these focused customer requirements into specific, quantifiable product requirements. (How can the product give the customers what they want?)

- Drives these product requirements into specific values and parameters for components, materials, and production operations. (How much of each element of the product requirements should be designed in, and in what fashion?)

Backing up a bit, let's ask ourselves how the customer's needs, concerns, and desires are identified. Successful users of QFD employ a wide variety of methods to capture the voice of the customer. This includes focus groups, opinion surveys, and other kinds of traditional market research techniques.

Within the world of QFD, however, there's more to it than asking the customers what they want—because *they won't tell you everything they want*. And that's because some things they take for granted, and other things they're not yet conscious of. Example: Ask one hundred people what they want in a car and probably none of them will tell you they want four wheels, an automatic starter, windshield wipers, or even a windshield. They assume those things will be there with any new car they'll buy.

Professor Noriaki Kano, who has written extensively about quality in Japan, talks about three kinds of quality as it relates to customers. See Figure 6-5.

THREE KINDS OF QUALITY, AS PERCEIVED BY THE CUSTOMER
1. Expected
2. Expressed
3. Exciting

FIGURE 6-5.

The first is *expected* quality, and that's what we've just seen. The customers simply assume that a given feature (e.g., windshield wipers) will be there, and thus they don't talk about it.

They do talk about the next one, *expressed* quality. Good handling, 0 to 60 in less than ten seconds, and lack of rust and rattles would be in this category.

The third, *exciting* quality, is like the first. It's not mentioned by the customers either—but for a different reason: They aren't yet aware of its existence. Exciting quality is the "Ah-ha!" It's "Isn't that great!" It's "They think of everything." The Sony Walkman, when it was first introduced, fit this characteristic to a T.

Back to automobiles, here's a small example from a few years ago: coffee cup holders. I've heard of people who bought cars very different from what they intended—simply because the car had a cup holder. It was an exciting feature; these customers felt the car designers really understood how they used their vehicles. (Today, cup holders in cars no longer qualify as an exciting quality. Most people now know about them. The cups have moved into the expressed quality area and would probably be mentioned in market research studies. A likely scenario: Ten years from now, all cars will have them. They'll be expected quality and won't even be mentioned.)

Another example, this time a big one: the Mazda Miata. Five or ten years ago, market research studies would have turned up almost no one who said they wanted a 1950s-type British roadster that cost less than fifteen thousand dollars and didn't break down frequently. Today a lot more people are buying them than would have asked for them then.

To get the exciting quality dimensions into the product design process, companies use not only the standard market research tools, but engage in close consultation with key customers, dealers, and distributors; capture input from users of competitive products; and, within the company, get involved in multifunctional brainstorming sessions.

By now you may be saying, "So what else is new? We've been doing good market research for years, as well as some of those other things you mentioned. And we're pretty good at Value Analysis and Value Engineering. Sounds to me as though we're already doing QFD."

Well, perhaps you are already doing it. On the other hand, probably not, because the number of QFD users in North America and Europe is very small. While many aspects of QFD are nothing new, it brings to the product design process a structure and a rigor not normally present.

Let's take a brief look at the mechanics of QFD. This simplified example is from a fine book by Bill Eureka and Nancy Ryan of the American Supplier Institute,ᴸ wherein they describe how QFD might be used in designing a cup of coffee.

Let's say that market research and other techniques have defined what makes up an excellent cup of coffee. These are the customer requirements, what the customers want. In QFD terms, they're the "whats." See Figure 6-6.

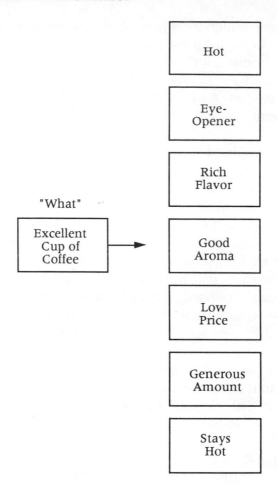

FIGURE 6-6.[2]

The QFD process then converts customer requirements into design requirements. This is done by translating the customers' words into design requirements, i.e., how the product will meet the customers' needs. These are the "hows" of QFD. See Figure 6-7.

Also, Figure 6-7 shows symbols depicting the relationships between "what items" and "how items." The how items begin to define product specifications. This is furthered by adding items

"How" Items

"What" Items	Serving Temperature	Amount of Caffeine	Flavor Component	Flavor Intensity	Aroma Component	Aroma Intensity	Sale Price	Volume	Temperature After Serving
Hot	◎								O
Eye-Opener	O	O							
Rich Flavor	△	△	◎	O					
Good Aroma					◎	O			
Low Price							◎	O	
Generous Amount							O	◎	
Stays Hot	O								◎

△ Weak
O Medium
◎ Strong

FIGURE 6-7.[3]

defining "how much." They're shown on the bottom of the matrix in Figure 6-8.

The "how much" items are quantified expressions of the "hows." They're addressed after the "hows" are determined. They give focus to ensure that the "hows" are being met, and serve as target values in the design process.

The basic QFD matrix is sometimes called the "House of Quality," and a look at Figure 6-9 will show why. The "roof" has been added, and this shows the correlation between "how items." For

"How" Items

"What" Items	Serving Temperature	Amount of Caffeine	Flavor Component	Flavor Intensity	Aroma Component	Aroma Intensity	Sale Price	Volume	Temperature After Serving
Hot	◎								O
Eye-Opener	O	O							
Rich Flavor	△	△	◎	O					
Good Aroma					◎	O			
Low Price							◎	O	
Generous Amount							O	◎	
Stays Hot	O								◎
△ Weak O Medium ◎ Strong	120-140° F	—— ppm	Established by Judges	Established by Judges	Established by Judges	Established by Judges	Less than $.25	Greater than 12 fl. Oz.	110-125° F

"How Much" Items

FIGURE 6-8.[4]

example, there is a strong positive correlation between Flavor Component and Aroma Component. If it tastes good, it will probably also smell good; improving one will tend to improve the other. That makes it easy.

On the other hand, negative correlations are difficult. One exists between Sale Price and Volume; these two are in conflict because a larger serving will cost more and tend to push up the price. Negative correlations often call for a great deal of study and for hard choices to be made.

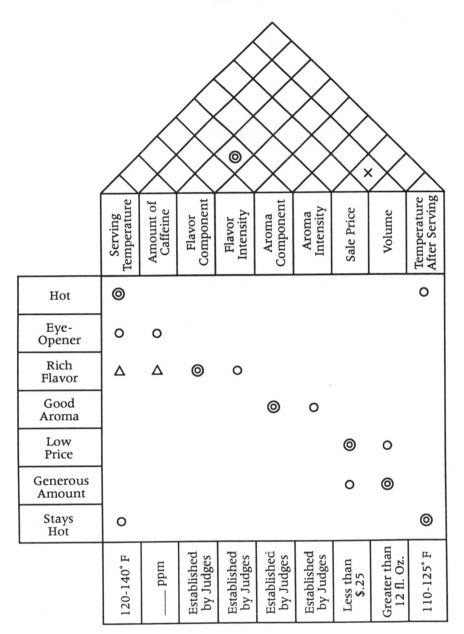

FIGURE 6-9.[5]

In this introductory treatment of Quality Function Deployment, we've only been able to scratch the surface. People who've successfully used QFD have found that it brings both a structure and insights to the development process that's extremely valuable.

DESIGN FOR MANUFACTURABILITY

"He who launches first wins." Not always the case, but certainly a credo to live by. By way of amplification, let's look at the results of a study by McKinsey & Company, as shown in Figure 6-10.

This is an example from a high-tech industry, where the product life cycles are quite short. Comparable data in another industry may not show such a dramatic picture, but chances are that this phenomenon will apply. For most industries, being first to the

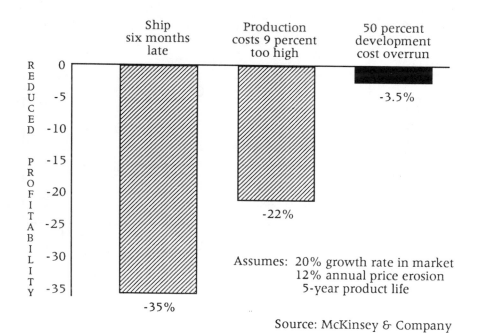

FIGURE 6-10.

market with a new product can result in substantially higher market share and greater profitability over the life of the product—and avoids the stigma of having a "me-too" product.

For many winning companies, Design for Manufacturability is the tool of choice. It stands in sharp contrast to the traditional "over-the-wall" approach, where certain people make the up-front decisions and then toss them over the wall into Manufacturing. It goes something like this:

PRODUCT DESIGN   (speaking to Manufacturing): "Here, make this."

MARKETING: "By the first of next month."

FINANCE: "For less than fifty dollars."

Concurrent Engineering

The concurrent engineering aspect of DFM is 180 degrees different from "over the wall." It involves operational people heavily in product design and development. Companies that involve manufacturing, purchasing, and supplier people early and intensively in the design process can develop better products and bring them to market more quickly, at lower cost and with higher quality. Thus, **MANUFACTURING, PURCHASING, AND SUPPLIER PEOPLE NEED TO PLAY AN EARLY AND INTENSIVE ROLE IN NEW PRODUCT DESIGN.** This intense and early involvement of operations people and suppliers is one of the hallmarks of DFM. See Figure 6-11.

It may be easier now to see why some companies call this Concurrent Engineering or Simultaneous Engineering. The essence of this is not only to involve production and supply people early in the design process, but also *to start actual procurement and production.* This is one way the DFM approach helps companies to launch new products in less time, to get to the market "firstest with the mostest."

The result is a multiple bang for the buck. New products get to

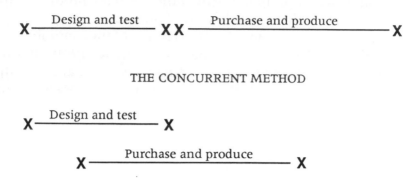

FIGURE 6-11.

market faster; they also get to market at lower cost and with higher quality. Due to early involvement by operations people, the products are easier to make (lower cost) and easier to make correctly (higher quality).

Okay, so it's a good deal—but is it easy to do? Of course not. If it were easy, we'd all be doing it already. Now let's ask ourselves several more questions. Of the two approaches shown in Figure 6-11, which requires more communications and more organizational competence? DFM, certainly. And the bad news is that most organizations lack the communication skills and competence required. The good news is that getting started with DFM can help a company:

- Start to improve its product introduction capabilities almost immediately.

- Begin to develop those skills and competence necessary to bring about a first-rate product launch.

Both of these changes can happen simultaneously. The learning curve applies here.

Let's ask ourselves another question: Which of these approaches is riskier? The obvious answer is DFM. After all, it calls for buying material and starting production before the final design is nailed down. After all, a design change could obsolete some material already purchased.

I submit that the obvious answer here may also be the incorrect one. The serial method—design it all, then buy and build—may in fact carry more risk, for the following reasons:

1. As the total organization—Product Design, Manufacturing, Purchasing, suppliers, *and* Marketing—starts to excel at the overlapped method, the chances for a major design change late in the process diminish. Hence the risk is lessened.

2. The serial method increases time-to-market, and that can be very expensive, as we saw in Figure 6-11.

3. The costs involved in being late to the marketplace will often heavily outweigh the costs an infrequent scrappage of material. Further, companies proficient at DFM often experience much less—or zero—design-caused obsolescence than before. This is due largely to the early involvement of production and supply people, who help to "bulletproof" the design early, rather than discover the problems only after the start of production.

DFM Mechanics

Geoffrey Boothroyd and Peter Dewhurst, two creative British gentlemen now at the University of Rhode Island, have developed a structured process to help people develop products that are easier to manufacture and assemble. It's done via a series of checklists, which help to focus the designers' attention on the economic aspects of the product they're creating.

This approach is computer-based and represents the mechanics of Design for Manufacturability. Within the software are the capabilities for designers to know, as the development process proceeds, the amount of cost they've designed in so far. It directs them toward easy-to-build designs, which will take less time to manufacture on the plant floor. It helps them use fewer parts.

Since you may be more familiar with Manufacturing Resource

Planning than with Design for Manufacturability, the following analogy may be helpful: The Boothroyd/Dewhurst methodology is to DFM as the software is to MRP II. It's an important piece, enabling people to improve their job performance.

TRADE-OFF ALERT: The conventional wisdom says trade-offs are a fact of life in designing products, and in most situations that's true. But it doesn't apply all the time. Take an example from the world of automobiles. It used to be that cars that offered great handling, rapid acceleration, and high top speeds were small, uncomfortable, unreliable, expensive, or all of the above.

Not anymore. Today certain cars offer all the performance most drivers could ever want, along with comfort, reliability, and the ability to seat four or five people comfortably. Included here are the European sedans. Less expensive examples include the Ford Taurus SHO, the Nissan Maxima, and the Honda Civic EX 4-Door Sedan, which has a performance envelope approaching those of cars costing two to three times as much. These sedans perform like sports cars; the earlier trade-offs have gone away.

In the 1950s, airplanes were able to go fast, approaching the speed of sound, but could carry only one or two people. Today it's commonplace for a plane carrying hundreds of people to fly at Mach .9. Today's trade-off is to carry three-hundred-plus people and cruise at Mach 3. It can't be done. But it will, during most of our lifetimes. Today's trade-off will go away.

Portable computers went from "luggables" (at around twenty-five pounds) to laptops (about fifteen pounds) to notebook computers (six pounds or less). At the same time, the power in those computers was *increasing*. Each new "generation" of portable computer eliminated a layer of weight/power trade-off.

Here's the point: The zero trade-off mind-set applies not only to improving a company's processes, it also applies to developing new products. Of course, it's impossible to ever achieve—literally—zero trade-offs in product design. But people can have a vision that drives them toward zero trade-off products. If a company can eliminate product trade-offs faster than the competition, it'll be at a big advantage.

Let's wrap up our discussion of new product development with another look at the office furniture people from Michigan.

Excellence in Action:

Steelcase Inc., Grand Rapids, Michigan

The "pyramid" rises starkly out of a restored prairie south of Grand Rapids. Reminiscent of a Mayan temple, or perhaps a huge spaceship, the Steelcase Corporate Development Center is a dramatic statement of the company's commitment to customer-driven product design.

As Steelcase grew to be the world's largest manufacturer of office furniture, so did its need for top-flight design people—and for space to house them. The company had begun digging the foundation for a new Product Development building, but stopped when the management team had second thoughts. They said, "Why are we putting up a traditional building to do product development in the same old way? We've never been as good at launching new products as I feel we could be."

Construction was halted. The architects went back to the drawing boards, and the result was a building uniquely designed to foster a high degree of interaction and teamwork among the people who work inside.

One indication of Steelcase's customer focus is the parking lot. The reserved parking spaces nearest the door are the requisite spots for handicapped people. However, unlike at virtually all other commercial buildings, the next spaces are not reserved for executives, the employee of the month, the company van, or visitors. They're reserved for *customers*.

Customers "work" in this building. They're present every day, along with a broad mix of outside design people, dealers, architects, suppliers, and Steelcase employees.

Some of the Steelcase people working in the pyramid are product engineers, marketing people, and buyers—all part of the Research Development and Industrial Design departments. But many are not. The multifunction development teams include people "on loan" from a wide range of departments, including Quality Assurance, Engineering, and Manufacturing. In some cases, one of the manufacturing people on the design team will be a production associate.

A typical team will first be located at the pyramid and will remain there until their product nears pilot production. At that point, the entire team moves from the pyramid to the plant where production will occur. They'll stay together through early production, at which time most of the members will return to their home departments.

Thanks to this intensely team-focused approach, and to the effective use of the kinds of tools we've discussed in this chapter, Steelcase's time-to-market has been cut in half. It's gone from three years to eighteen months, and is targeted to reach 10 months within the next few years. Product acceptance in the marketplace, which has always been excellent, is getting even better. And not only in North America and Europe.

Example: In Japan, one of the "national pastimes" is playing a game called Pachinko. These are coin-operated devices, not unlike pinball machines, typically located in a Pachinko parlor. It's big business in Japan: more than 3 million machines are presently installed, yielding $82 billion in annual sales. The game is played sitting on a stool.

After a while, the stools can become uncomfortable. The Pachinko people concluded that, if the players could be made more comfortable, they would play longer and thus spend more money. Looking for a solution, they found themselves doing business with an office furniture company located in the American Midwest.

Steelcase, with its ability to capture the voice of the customer, and to develop new products quickly, and to have superb quality and delivery at the right price, won the order. Jerry Hekker, who runs Steelcase's seating business unit, says: "Just a few years ago, we couldn't have captured that business. Today we're able to do it, and we see some exciting derivative product possibilities developing from this experience."

Steelcase, as of this writing, has shipped tens of thousands of very comfortable chair/stool units to the Orient, to be used by the Pachinko players of Japan.

STRATEGIC CHECKUP

- Do the company's people widely view new product introductions as positive opportunities to win in the marketplace, or are they dreaded for the problems they typically bring?

- Does the company lead or lag the competition in launching new products?

- Does the company consistently launch new products in less time than it did two years ago? Are there plans for further reductions?

- Does the company have a formal process to embed the voice of the customer in new product design?

- Are manufacturing, purchasing, and supplier people involved early and intensively in new product development?

Developing and successfully launching new products, routinely, equates to continuous innovation. But a healthy, robust, competitive company also needs to excel at the continuous improvement of its processes. That's next.

CHAPTER SEVEN

Continuous Improvement— The Conscience

"The processes involved in continuous improvement generate a creative discontent with the status quo. This makes it unacceptable for the company to rest on its laurels, and forces it to improve."

Just-in-Time, Total Quality Control, and Benchmarking form the basis for continuous improvement, but there's great confusion about how they fit together. One of the causes of this confusion is the blurred distinction between Total Quality Control (TQC) and Total Quality Management (TQM). Total Quality Management equates to overall operational excellence. Total Quality Control is a technology, based on the assurance of quality at the point where the work is performed. It also includes the set of tools and techniques that enable people to solve problems and thereby improve quality—Statistical Process Control, Cause-and-Effect Diagrams, Pareto Charting, Root Cause Analysis, and many others.

MYTHS ABOUT JUST-IN-TIME

Another source of confusion here is the mythology that's sprung up around Just-in-Time. For example:

Myth: Just-in-Time is an inventory-reduction program.

Myth: Just-in-Time is a scheduling system.

Myth: Just-in-Time is all about daily deliveries from suppliers.

Unfortunately, there's enough truth in each of these myths to make them appear valid. However, they miss the mark; they fail to communicate the essence of the process, which is continuous improvement via the elimination of waste. As such, these myths can lead people to do the wrong things, one of which is doing nothing. Doing nothing about Just-in-Time is the wrong thing to do, because it's essential—for virtually all companies. Let's see why.

THE ESSENCE OF CONTINUOUS IMPROVEMENT

During a trip to Japan a few years ago, I spent some time with a gentleman from Japanese academia, Professor Jinichiro (Jim) Nakane of Waseda University. One of the things we talked about was the difference between small steps and quantum leaps.

Jim went to the blackboard and made the following points: "In America, you people are very good at quantum leaps—major improvements via large projects." See Figure 7-1.

"In Japan," Jim said, "we seem to be effective in making frequent, small improvements." See Figure 7-2.

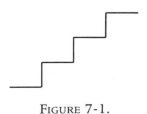

FIGURE 7-1.

FIGURE 7-2.

He went on to say: "In Japan we need to improve our ability to manage large projects, to make quantum leaps. In America, if I may say so, you might improve your ability to make small improvement steps, on a continuous basis." It made sense to me. Competitive advantage will go to the company—and country—that is skilled in both areas.

Here's how it's often happened in North America, using one of my prior employers as an example. At a given point, my company decided to reduce costs. We launched a cost-reduction project as a major initiative for the fiscal year. We had buttons, banners, slogans, and all the trimmings. The goal: reduce costs by X percent. By the end of the year, guess what? We hit our objective. We reduced costs by X percent.

Well, what did we do for the next year? We wanted to increase quality. So, another major project, this one to improve quality by Y percent. We did it.

The following year? Another project, this one to reduce inventories by Z percent.

In retrospect, we were *way above average*. We typically accomplished what we set out to do. We avoided the "flavor of the month" syndrome, where one initiative follows another so closely that the earlier ones can't be finished properly and therefore aren't successful. But, even with our success, our approach was not the best.

One problem with this method is that it's sporadic. Another is that too often we focused on the numbers and not on the elimination of the source of the problems.

A good example is inventory reduction, which is a lot like losing weight. Most people can lose weight—temporarily—via a crash diet. But it comes back. Most companies can reduce their inventory (or costs or defects)—temporarily—via a crash program. But it comes back. The "yo-yo" effect—down, then up, down, then up—occurs in business as well as in our personal efforts for weight loss.

In winning companies—in North America and Europe as well as in Japan—people do it differently. They get up in the morning, get cleaned up, dress, eat breakfast, and go to work; they reduce costs, cut lead times, increase quality, and raise productivity—as a *normal part of their jobs*. They do the same thing the next day, and the day after, and the day after that. That's how companies are able to generate dozens, in some cases hundreds, of implemented employee suggestions per employee per year, as we saw earlier in our discussion of People Empowerment.

"We focus internally on what we call a constant state of discontent," says Larry Osterwise, General Manager of the IBM plant that won the Malcolm Baldrige National Quality Award. "When you think you are the best, that's when you have to worry about getting better. We learned from the Baldrige that we are pretty good. But we realized that the opportunity for improvement is greater than we ever anticipated."[1]

To those companies that haven't learned to function in a continuous improvement mode, the magnitude of the competitive challenge is enormous. But I'm not sure that it has everyone's attention. Here's an example. Referring to Lexus automobiles, a recent *Fortune* magazine article[2] stated: "Toyota turns out luxury sedans with Mercedes-like quality using *one-sixth* the labor Mercedes does." (The emphasis is theirs.) To round out the picture, I might point out that Toyota is not known for being more heavily automated than most other auto makers.

A few days later I read the following in *Automotive Week* magazine[3]: "The head of Mercedes-Benz's car division realizes his company must cut costs and improve productivity if it is to be competitive with the Japanese. [He] said a study shows his company has to make a *30 percent improvement* in both areas and said Mercedes has set a *three to five-year* timetable to meet those goals." (Emphasis mine.)

Well, if Toyota does in fact have a six-fold advantage in direct labor productivity, a 30 percent improvement by Mercedes will hardly put a dent in Toyota's lead—even if Mercedes were shooting at a sitting target. But they're not. Toyota lives and breathes continuous improvement; within three to five years, they may have improved by 20 or 30 percent—or more.

Here's *Fortune* again: "In short, Toyota is the best carmaker in the world. And it keeps getting better." A word of warning to the European auto industry: It's later than you think.

So how do they do it, the Toyotas and the Sonys and the Toshibas? They do it the same way that Xerox and Steelcase and Hewlett-Packard and many others do it in the U.S. They don't do it with "programs," they do it with process—the process that we call "continuous improvement," and the Japanese call "kaizen."

The heart of continuous improvement is Just-in-Time (JIT) and Total Quality Control (TQC), working together. They're two sides of the same coin; using them together, in concert, generates far greater results than using only one or the other.

Either one, by itself, can be helpful to a company. For example, some organizations have implemented Total Quality without Just-in-Time and received substantial benefits. What most of them did not do, however, is embed continuous improvement into the company as a way of life.

Implementing Just-in-Time without TQC is even less desirable. Without TQC's problem-solving tools, Just-in-Time can become an exercise in frustration—uncovering problems but not being able to solve them well. Bruce Harvey, during his years at Hewlett-Packard, learned that "Just-in-Time without Total Quality Control, or vice versa, is like standing on one leg. You can do it, but the effort is much greater. And you can't walk or run very well." Just-in-Time and Total Quality Control, when implemented together, yield far greater results than any independent quality-improvement program." **CONTINUOUS IMPROVEMENT REQUIRES BOTH JUST-IN-TIME (THE CATALYST TO UNCOVER WASTE) AND TOTAL QUALITY CONTROL (THE SET OF TOOLS TO ELIMINATE WASTE).**

Let's see how it happens.

JUST-IN-TIME: THE DRIVER

Earlier we saw some Just-in-Time mythology: "Just-in-Time is an inventory-reduction program." "Just-in-Time is a scheduling system." "Just-in-Time is all about daily deliveries from suppliers." Let's set the record straight.

First, Just-in-Time is not a program, it's a process, a way of driving change throughout a manufacturing company. To call Just-in-Time a program demeans it. (Some call it a philosophy, but I find that term a bit too full blown in this context. Aristotle, Kant, Descartes, and perhaps Adam Smith were philosophers. The inventors of Just-in-Time—Henry Ford of the Ford Motor Company and Taiichi Ohno from Toyota—were brilliant men; philosophers they weren't.)

Second, inventory reduction is only one of many things made possible by Just-in-Time. Inventory reduction is a by-product of the JIT process working well. To view Just-in-Time solely, or even primarily, as a tool to reduce inventories devalues it.

Third, there's much more to Just-in-Time than scheduling. True, the Just-in-Time technique called kanban has a scheduling role, but it's only one part of the larger technology. To imply that Just-in-Time deals mainly with scheduling devalues it.

Last, Just-in-Time is not an activity confined solely to suppliers. It involves the entire company (and ultimately its customers), and to imply otherwise devalues it.

Well, if it isn't those things, just what is it? What's Just-in-Time all about? Here's what it means, boiled down to the essentials:

Just-in-Time means forced elimination of waste.

Waste is that which does not add value to the product.

Examples of waste, of non-value-adding activities, include:

- Separate inspection steps. (They do not alter the item, do not add to its value.)

- Sitting inventory. (Except for certain items—beverages and foodstuffs come to mind—true value is not being added to items sitting in inventory. Value is added only when the inventory is moving to or through the production processes to the customers.)

- Making more of an item than is needed at that time. (If we make more than we need, we'll have to move it, store it, count it, pay taxes on it, insure it, and hope we need it sometime in the future.)

But there's another problem with this. Let's take the case of the Acme Widget Company. (Acme is a fictitious firm, a composite of several different real ones; no one company could be this misguided. Or could it?) Acme launched into Just-in-Time fixated solely on the above viewpoint: to eliminate non-value-adding activities. Here's what happened:

1. They eliminated the finished-goods inventory, because they recognized that sitting inventory doesn't add value to the product. As a result, customer delivery performance plummeted.

2. They stopped inspecting, because separate inspection steps do not add value to the product. Therefore, many of the products they did manage to ship were of poor quality.

3. They made only what they needed at the time. Because of this, people in the plant had to make very short production runs and were spending most of their time setting up equipment instead of making product.

Isn't this great? They took a stab at Just-in-Time and generated the following results: Shipments were down, the customers were unhappy, market share was slipping, plant efficiency went way down, and the company got a bad reputation for quality.

The culprit in the above example is the failure to understand the nature of waste—of these non-value-adding activities.

Waste breaks out into two categories: necessary and unnecessary. Eliminating unnecessary waste is the easy part of Just-in-Time.

The hard part is to convert necessary waste into unnecessary; once that happens, getting rid of it can be much simpler.

To say it another way: Most often Just-in-Time doesn't directly eliminate waste, it eliminates the *need* for waste.

The Just-in-Time Process

Bill Sandras, formerly a key player in a number of JIT implementations within Hewlett-Packard, has developed an excellent way to communicate the real essence of this process for continuous improvement.[4] It's shown in Figure 7-3.

The top box on the diagram says: SELECT AN AREA FOR IMPROVEMENT. Let's say that I'm a supervisor in one of your plants, a foreman in charge of a production department. My name is Tom, and I report to you. Your name is Boss. You feel that my department might be a good candidate for waste elimination.

Next box, the diamond: IS WASTE GREATER THAN ZERO? You ask me about my run quantities, how many of a given item I run at a time.

TOM: "Well, Boss, for most of our items, we like to run about twenty [or two hundred or two thousand or twenty thousand—whatever] at a time."
BOSS: "Why do you do that? Because you need all twenty at once?"
TOM: "No, not really."

At that point, I have answered "Yes" to the question "Is waste greater than zero?" Think about it: If we make more than what our immediate needs call for, we have to move it, store it, count it, insure it, pay taxes on it, and run the risk of its going obsolete or being damaged. In virtually all companies, none of those things adds value to the product.

The next diamond: IS THE PROCESS ECONOMICAL?

BOSS: "Why do you run more than you need?"

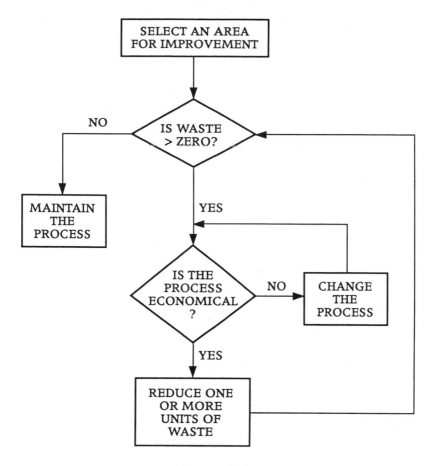

FIGURE 7-3.

TOM: "Twenty's a good quantity to run because of our setup times."

I have just answered "Yes" to the question "Is the process economical?" This question refers to the current process, in this case making twenty at a time.

Next box: REDUCE ONE OR MORE UNITS OF WASTE. Please note those words. They do not say:

• Let well enough alone.

- If it ain't broke, don't fix it.

- We're doin' good.

- Let's create a committee to study the problem.

It says, "Reduce one or more units of waste." Let's say we do that. We cut the order quantities from twenty down to nineteen. Follow the line coming out of that box up to the first diamond. It asks: IS WASTE GREATER THAN ZERO? Well, nineteen is still more than we need at the time. That's a yes. Fall through to the next diamond: IS THE PROCESS ECONOMICAL?

BOSS: "Tom, how are things going now that you're running nineteen at a time?"
TOM: "It's okay."

That's a yes. Go to the next box: REDUCE ONE OR MORE UNITS OF WASTE. Cut the run sizes to eighteen.

BOSS: "How are you doing at eighteen?"
TOM: "Not too bad."

That's a yes. Take another one away. (Please note: At this point we've reduced the run quantities by 10 percent without having to do anything extraordinary. The attendant reduction in inventory represents unnecessary waste.)

BOSS: "How's it going at seventeen?"
TOM: "It's starting to squeak a bit, but we're getting by."

That's a yes. Take another one away.

BOSS: "How's sixteen?"
TOM: "Lousy! I was afraid this was going to happen. You're nickel-and-dimin' us to death. We're spending too much time changing over. It's getting tougher and tougher to hit our output targets. Give us a break and add at least one or two back in."

Sound like a no to you? It sure does to me. And it is. And the worst thing we can do here is go along with what Tom's asking. If we put one or two back into the order quantity, what have we just done? We have institutionalized the waste, and that's not the road to competitive success—but possibly to extinction.

Most companies use inventory like a drug. When they encounter a problem, they give themselves a "hit" of inventory and that makes the pain go away. This can be lethal. Instead, we need to transform the "necessary waste" of making sixteen at a time into unnecessary waste so we can eliminate it.

A "no" answer sends us to the right, to the box labeled CHANGE THE PROCESS. Which process to change? At this point, what needs to be changed is the setup time. Tom's unhappy because he's spending too much time on changeovers and not enough time producing.

Let's say we do that, we attack the setup times in Tom's department. We cut them in half. Back up to the diamond: IS WASTE GREATER THAN ZERO? It sure is. Fall through: IS THE CURRENT PROCESS ECONOMICAL?

BOSS: "How's it going now, Tom?"
TOM: "Super! No problem. We making smaller lots, but we're spending much less time setting up than we ever did."

That's a yes. Take another one away, down to fifteen, and repeat the process. Over and over again. And what might happen when they get down to around fourteen is that someone other than Tom might begin to yell.

That someone may be the quality-control people. You see, Tom's now running smaller batches, which means more batches per unit of time, which means more samples and inspections and tests by QC. In this example, the number of batches in Tom's department will have increased by about 40 percent. What hasn't increased is the number of QC inspectors, and that's what the QC manager is asking for: more inspectors. In effect, she's saying "No" to the question "Is the current process economical?" The process she's talking about is inspection. This can lead companies to replace separate inspection steps (which do not add value to the product) with certain of the tools within Total Quality Control, such as Statistical Process Control or other kinds of in-line methods, with operator responsibility for assuring quality. (More on this later in this chapter.)

When the run quantities get down to ten or so, who might start to scream? It could be the people in the stockrooms and warehouse. They're having to kit (or load or disburse) twice as many orders to Tom's department. Well, we certainly don't want to hire more people for the warehouse because issuing materials from stores does not add value to the product.

This can lead companies into techniques like point-of-use storage, where the materials and components are stocked in the production departments and the production people are held accountable for inventory record accuracy.

How does the one-less-at-a-time process work outside of the plant floor? Answer: wonderfully. One example is lead-time reduction. This is such an important item because unnecessarily long lead times impact delivery performance, flexibility, and inventories. The one-less-at-a-time approach can be used to directly reduce customer lead times not only within the plant but also in the order entry process, in the Credit Department, in Purchasing, and at their suppliers. Lead-time reduction is win-win-win-win. Everybody is better off.

This, then, is the essence of Just-in-Time:

1. JIT forces the identification of waste, so that it can be eliminated. In effect, Just-in-Time says: "If everything's okay, take another one away." It's relentless. It will not let you rest.

2. Waste is being removed in very small increments—"one less at a time." Making very gradual changes allows us to not harm current operations while the improvement process is going on. Therefore, it's no risk and enables continuous improvement to become a normal way of operating the business.

Kanban

One of the techniques within Just-in-Time to make it work is called "kanban" (rhymes with bonbon). It's a Japanese word which, loosely translated, means an authorization to produce or deliver. Let's see what Bill Sandras has to say about kanban:

> The kanban technique is similar to the process once used by the milkman as he delivered milk to a home. When the milkman arrived, he would immediately see how many empty milk bottles were left on the porch. Two empty containers authorized him to deliver two full bottles. If there was one regular and one chocolate empty, he'd leave one regular and one chocolate milk. Those empty milk bottles were his authorization to leave more. No bottle, no milk.
>
> Kanban works the same way, as a signal to replace what has been used. If the kanban authorization is present, you act. If not, you don't. Kanban is, therefore, a way of controlling inventory. As such, it is also an ideal method of exposing problems or opportunities for change.[5]

TOTAL QUALITY CONTROL

This is the other side of the continuous-improvement coin. Within TQC are contained the tools to facilitate waste elimination. See Figure 7-4.

You may be thinking: "Isn't it possible to eliminate waste without using TQC?" We may have just seen an example of that—setup reduction. TQC may not have a large role in that specific improvement activity. There may be others like that.

By the same token, it's possible to uncover waste without using the JIT, "one-less-at-a-time" method. Implementing good-quality

JUST-IN-TIME/TOTAL QUALITY CONTROL

Two sides of the same coin

Uncover waste   Eliminate cause

FIGURE 7-4.

processes in an organization will result in large amounts of waste identification and elimination.

For competitive purposes, though, it's not good enough. Either one, by itself, will help a great deal. Neither one, by itself, will result in continuous improvement becoming a way of life within the company.

For a definition of Total Quality Control, let's go right to the source, to the man who coined the phrase. No, it's not Deming or Juran or Crosby or somebody from Japan; it's Armand V. Feigenbaum, at the time with the General Electric Company:

> Total Quality Control is an effective system for integrating the quality-development, quality-maintenance, and quality-improvement efforts of the various groups in an organization so as to enable production and service at the most economical levels which allow for full customer satisfaction.[6]

Some key words from that definition:

Total—refers to all products, all departments, all functions, all processes, all components, all materials.

Integrating—as is the case with other superb tools, it helps to tie together diverse functions and activities.

Quality-development, quality-maintenance, quality improvement—refers to quality as a constant and ongoing process: Design it in, live by it, and improve it.

Various groups in the organization—means quality is multifunctional. It's everyone's job, not just the job of the Quality Control Department.

Economical—quality is not expensive: it is cost effective.

Full customer satisfaction—the name of the game.

Feigenbaum's words were written in 1961. Unfortunately, it took most of North American industry until the 1980s to start to pay attention to his statement and others like it.

We've already talked about quality in earlier chapters. Now we need to go further. We need to look at some bedrock concepts and tools to round out the picture.

Cost of Quality

This powerful concept—Cost of Quality—addresses all the costs a company incurs by not doing it right the first time. One obvious component of total quality costs includes failure costs: things like scrap and rework, warranty costs, field repair, and the like. Many companies spend lots of money here. However, there's more. Appraisal costs cover inspection and testing, and in many cases this can be significant. Lastly, prevention costs include education and training, quality audits, and process changes to enable higher quality. Frequently, far too little is spent here.

The Cost of Quality equals:

appraisal costs
+
failure costs
+
prevention costs

If you haven't heard this statistic before, you might have a hard time accepting it, but it's a fact: The Cost of Quality in many companies will range between 15 to 20 percent of total sales—or more.[7]

Total Quality Control, pursued properly, has resulted in huge reductions to companies' Cost of Quality—from 25 percent to 5 percent, from 30 percent to 3 percent. Almost invariably, appraisal costs and failure costs plummet while prevention costs may increase several times over. Since most companies, pre-TQC, spent big bucks on appraisal and failure and far too little on prevention, this is a happy situation indeed. It's what enabled Phil Crosby to say, correctly, that quality is free.

Here's a company that has lived and breathed quality—in its fullest sense—since the 1970s.

Excellence in Action:

THE TENNANT COMPANY, MINNEAPOLIS, MINNESOTA

The Tennant Company, a manufacturer of industrial sweepers and scrubbers, became so good at quality that they wrote a book about it.[8] And that book was so well received that they wrote another one.[9]

Tennant, already with a reputation for top-quality products, started on their "quality journey" back in 1979 in a particularly interesting way. Roger Hale, CEO and President, tells it this way: "During my visits with our Japanese joint-venture partner in the late 1970s, I had been hearing complaints—sometimes bitter complaints—about hydraulic leaks in our most successful machines. Back home, I began asking questions: Why were the hydraulic leaks happening only in the machines we sent to Japan and not in those we were selling in the U.S.? . . .

"As it turned out, the leaks weren't just happening in Japan. The machines we sold here at home were leaking too. The difference was that U.S. customers accepted the leaks. If a drop of oil appeared on a freshly polished floor, they simply wiped it up. In Japan, the leak was cause for complaint. Japanese customers expected better quality. . . .

"At about the same time, we faced our first serious competition in Japan from the lift-truck division of Toyota when it announced its entry into the sweeper business. . . ."

Keep in mind: When it came to quality, these people were already above average. Their cost of quality in 1980 was 17 percent, substantially below the 20 to 30 percent range cited above. They made fine machines; they dominated their market.

The 1980s were a decade of enormous progress in quality improvement for Tennant. Several key reasons for their success were

1. Strong leadership and commitment from the top.

2. Lack of arrogance. Even though it was already an excellent company, it genuinely wanted to do better and *it was willing to learn*.

3. Hard work, lots of it, over an extended time.

By the mid-1980s, Just-in-Time had kicked in. This resulted in reduced space requirements, avoiding the need for a new plant and eliminating 35,000 square feet of a rental warehouse. It also provided the quality processes with more opportunities to eliminate waste.

By 1988, their cost of quality had dropped from 17 percent of sales to 2.5 percent. For Tennant, with about $200 million in sales, this represents $29 million in bottom-line benefits.

Another benefit: the absence of any significant Japanese presence in the American sweeper and scrubber market. My guess is it will continue that way for a long time to come.

But that's not all. Instead of the Japanese penetrating the American market, it's going the other way. Here's Bill Strang, Tennant's Director of Marketing: "We are doing well in the Japanese market. We have the largest share of the industrial cleaning equipment market and our business there is growing."

Source Assurance of Quality

One important aspect of TQC is to eliminate separate inspection steps (thereby reducing appraisal costs). Separate inspection steps don't add value to the product; they constitute waste and should be eliminated.

In most companies, prior to JIT/TQC, separate inspection steps are *necessary* waste. They don't add value to the product, but they must be taken until they can be replaced with something else. That "something else" must verify quality without being wasteful; as such, it will enable the necessary waste to become unnecessary.

Sometimes the necessary waste cannot be transformed into unnecessary waste. In some industries governmental requirements mandate that separate inspection steps occur. Examples abound in the aircraft business, and also in pharmaceuticals.

Except in those kinds of environments, this is where source assurance of quality enters the picture. By "source" I'm not referring only to suppliers; rather, it means the resource actually producing the item. Some people call it "in-line quality assurance." Individual production associates are held accountable for the quality of their production. Obviously, we can't hold people accountable for results until they have the appropriate skills and tools.

One of the primary tools is Statistical Process Control (SPC), which calls for checking the output of the process as it's being produced. Key variables (e.g., dimensions, potency, hardness/softness) are measured and compared against predetermined control (tolerance) limits. When the measurements indicate that the process is starting to drift out of control, the production associate has the authority to stop the process. He can then make an adjustment to the equipment, check the raw material for suitability, get help from a supervisor or technical specialist, or do whatever else is needed to get the process back into control.

In Japan, they refer to this technique as "andon" (which means "warning light" and refers to the flashing lights that alert people that a process has been shut down). This involves giving the individual production associate authority to stop the process. It sounds so logical, and it is. What could make less sense than producing items that are known to be defective?

Just because something's logical, though, doesn't mean that it will be easy to implement. In some plants there's a major cultural shift required to place that amount of authority in the hands of individual production associates. This cultural shift requires education and training, not only for the associates but also for the supervisor (for whom this change is sometimes more difficult than for the associates).

No matter what the technique is called, quality, must be assured at the source. In this new environment, the quality of production is the direct responsibility of the production associates, not of someone in a department called QC.

TRADE-OFF ALERT: Do you remember comedian Flip Wilson's character named Geraldine? One of her often-used lines was "The devil made me do it!" The implication was that it, whatever "it" was, was beyond her control.

Here's an industrial equivalent of Geraldine's mind-set. A quarter-century ago, when I was in the pharmaceutical business, we purchased organic chemicals from outside suppliers. Before they could ship to us, the suppliers had to perform chemical assays on the material and fill out lots of paperwork attesting to its quality.

When we received the material, the first thing we did was to assay the material and fill out lots of paperwork. Was there waste in this system? A whole lot. But we had no choice, or so we thought, because "the FDA [Food and Drug Administration] made us do it." In the pharmaceutical business, FDA regulations carry the force of law; compliance is not an option.

In the trade-off between compliance and waste reduction, you can guess which one came out on top. We complied, and thus lived with the waste and inefficiency. But that was twenty-five years ago.

Now, my friends in the pharmaceutical business tell me, the Food and Drug Administration has changed its regulations, thanks to some "encouragement" from enlightened companies in the industry. Under the proper conditions, the supplier's test results and paperwork are now sufficient and the confirming tests and documentation are no longer required.

Another trade-off, this one between regulatory compliance and non-value-adding activities, has been eliminated.

Mistake-Proofing

No less an authority than Shigeo Shingo maintains that Statistical Process Control is not the "be all and end all" of quality assurance.[10] Rather, the ultimate quality-assurance tool is mistake-proofing (in Japanese: *Poka-yoke*), which means to design the product and/or process so that it's *impossible* to make it other than exactly the *right* way.

Sound like pie in the sky? Examples of effective mistake-proofing abound in many industries, one being aircraft design. Murphy's Law, Variation #17—aircraft assembly and maintenance division—says: When in the course of human events it becomes possible to install a part into an airplane incorrectly, then

sooner or later someone will do just that.[11] Therefore a fundamental principle of aircraft design is (to have the parts go) together
only in the correct manner.

When there's only one way to do it, and that's the right way,
then it should no longer be necessary to inspect it, measure it, test
it, tweak it, or whatever.

In actual practice, many uses of mistake-proofing focus on the
production process as much as or more than on the product design.
The processes themselves are designed in a way to provide instant
feedback to detect abnormalities; in-line gauges, limit switches,
sensors, mechanical gates, and photoelectric cells are some of the
tools used here. Several other ones also come to mind—cross
footing of numbers from the world of accounting, and check digits
in data processing. And, hopefully without stretching the point too
much, we could include having an explicit strategy to bulletproof
the decision-making process. In this sense, the strategic filter
"mistake-proofs" one's decisions.

Is mistake-proofing always possible? No, not at all. And sometimes it's possible but not practical. In most companies, though,
opportunities for Poka-yoke abound—far more than would be
expected.

No discussion of quality would be complete without addressing a
very important item, one that has led many companies to get very
serious about total quality.

The Baldrige Award

An important part of the "quality renaissance" in the U.S. is the
Malcolm Baldrige National Quality Award. Its mission includes the
furthering of:

- Awareness of quality as an increasingly important element in
  competitiveness.

- Understanding of the requirements for quality excellence.

- Sharing of information on successful quality strategies and on
  the benefits derived from implementation of these strategies."[12]

Winning the Baldrige Award is very difficult, as there is only a handful of winners each year. Even submitting an application for the award involves a great deal of time and effort. Despite the intensity of the process, a Baldrige application will lead companies to improve their processes. And that's really the important objective: process improvement.

The Baldrige Award has been criticized for having so few winners. It seems to me, however, that most Baldrige applicants are winners; they come out of the process better than before.

Here's David Kearns, formerly the CEO at Xerox:

> We put about seventeen people on [the Baldrige submission] for a year during a time when huge cost pressures were on us. . . .
>
> But why go after the award? To rate yourself on a worldwide basis against the very best, and then use that information to build the future. There isn't any question in my mind that it's a highly worthwhile experience. . . .
>
> I would urge everybody . . . to go after the award, and I wouldn't worry about winning it.[13]

Another beneficial aspect to Baldrige: It's a successful joint venture between industry (funds, volunteers, information sharing) and government (it's coordinated by the U.S. Department of Commerce). We need more of these kinds of things in the U.S.—industry and government cooperating instead of hammering on each other.

Is there a downside to Baldrige? There may be. Many feel it's not sufficiently broad based; its scope is too narrow. Here are Jerry Bowles, publisher of *The Quality Executive* newsletter, and Joshua Hammond, President of the American Quality Foundation:

> The award's [popularity] masks a disturbing fact: Its standards of quality are not broad enough to keep American companies on the leading edge in the coming years. . . .
>
> The process is limited, and it ignores "forward" quality—developing new products, services, and markets. Companies focusing on technical quality but ignoring this are buying a one-way ticket on the extinction express.
>
> We are moving toward a global business environment in which

quality is a given; you can't stay in the game without it. The challenge for American companies is not to "out-Japanese the Japanese" on quality—that's a game we can't win. Companies must sharply improve their quality but then not just sit back and feel good about that. Quality is not enough.[14]

Exactly. That's what we've been saying throughout this book: Quality is only one competitive dimension, although often the most important one, along with delivery, flexibility, and the rest. Trying to compete on quality alone is like trying to fly an airplane on one wing—it's a ticket to extinction.

The Malcolm Baldrige National Quality Award, with its intense focus on customer satisfaction, is a winner. It's made a major contribution to the competitiveness of U.S. industry. But keep it in perspective. Quality alone is not enough.

BENCHMARKING

Within the arena of continuous improvement, it's important to have outside input about "what the other guys are doing." This can help to guide and shape a company's improvement initiatives in several important ways:

1. Get new ideas.

2. Learn what's possible.

3. Define how high the high bar really is.

4. Help to focus on what to work on.

Most companies stay aware of what the competition is doing. This includes gathering information on products, pricing, promotions, distribution methods, warranties, field service practices, and the like. Sources typically include field sales people, distributors, customers, trade shows, and industry publications.

On the other hand, not many companies have a formal process

to track Item 2—how well other companies are doing relative to themselves and vice versa. That process is called "benchmarking."

My colleague Pete Landry, a key player in the Xerox "renaissance" of the 1980s, defines benchmarking as "the continuous process of measuring our products, services, and practices against our toughest competitors or those companies renowned as leaders."

Much of a company's benchmarking is done against competitors, but not all. When Xerox wanted to benchmark their processes for warehousing, order picking, packing, and shipping, they looked beyond at their competition. They benchmarked against L. L. Bean, which is regarded as one of the leaders in those kinds of processes. It's a very large part of Bean's business. The point: If you look only within your industry, you may never get better than your best competitor. Looking outside, benchmarking against the best in class for a given function, can provide a company with opportunities to leapfrog the competition.

This benchmarking process, to be truly effective, needs to be ongoing. Pete Landry goes on to say: "If you're benchmarking against world-class companies, you can be assured that these companies have internalized the full meaning of 'continuous improvement' and their performance is improving every year. . . . Benchmarking is a discovery process and a learning experience. . . . Using benchmarking data, we develop plans and strategies to maintain positive gaps and close negative ones."

Let's link back to our discussion of people empowerment. We said that what's needed is to *create an environment that enables the people to make continuous improvements in what they do.* You see, it's difficult to empower people in a vacuum; they need something to be empowered about. That "something" is continuous improvement, in all its many forms. Continuous improvement won't happen without empowered people, at all levels in the organization; empowered people must be chartered—*and enabled*—to make continuous improvements.

STRATEGIC CHECKUP

- Are the company's people, at all levels, empowered to make continuous improvements?

- Do your Total Quality processes include a focused method, e.g., Just-in-Time, for uncovering waste?

- Does the company have a formal process for benchmarking against both competitors and best in class?

- Do the findings from your benchmarking activities serve to direct your continuous-improvement processes?

Coming up next: how to keep things coordinated and controlled on a daily, weekly, and monthly basis—things like shipping on time, hitting the sales plan and build plan, and keeping track of the dollars.

CHAPTER EIGHT

Tactical Planning and Control—The Central Nervous System

"These processes transmit signals from the brain throughout the entire organization. They're the 'neurological network' that ties together the many and varied components of the healthy, robust company."

Last year I was talking with one of my neighbors, who's an M.D. and thus not very familiar with manufacturing companies. I was trying to describe to him what I do for a living. I talked about how companies need to have linkage between their top-level strategic plans and the more detailed plans for procurement, production, and shipment of customer orders. I added that when these detailed plans were valid and realistic, then people could execute them, thus completing the linkage between top-level strategy and the day-to-day running of the business.

He was not impressed. He said, "You're telling me that's what you do for a living?"

"Yes," I replied.

"But it's so obvious. Don't all manufacturing companies operate this way?"

"No, Frank, they don't."

"A majority of them do it this way, surely?"

"I'm afraid not."

Frank, who owns stock in a number of major corporations, frowned and then asked: "Surely the larger manufacturing companies, the ones in the Fortune 500, all do it this way?"

"Nope. Some do; many don't."

"But why not?! It's so logical."

To see "why not," let's recognize that many manufacturing companies plan strategically; most companies do some form of tactical planning on a month-to-month, week-to-week, day-to-day basis; and all companies execute. Here's how it works out:

1. Not all companies do all three.

2. Of those companies that do all three, far fewer do all three well.

3. Even within the group that does all three well, the linkages are often weak. Frequently strategy is not linked tightly to the ongoing planning for sales, logistics, and production.

In many companies, there's a major deficiency in the tactical planning area. The primary tool of choice here is called Manufacturing Resource Planning (MRP II); while quite a few companies use it very well, many do not. (Distribution Resource Planning (DRP) also plays a role in tactical planning; we'll cover it in the chapter on the Supply Chain.)

MRP II is not strategic; it's tactical. It doesn't tell us where to drive the car; it tells us how. It tells us when to speed up and slow down, when to change lanes, where to get gas, where to eat, etc.

Companies need to plan well—at *all levels*—in order to execute well. Only when they execute well can they achieve their strategic goals, one of which is—or should be—to be the best in their industry at what's important to their customers.

When it's done correctly, strategy fits hand in glove with tactical planning and execution. First, there's linkage and coherence between the company's top-level strategic plans and the more detailed tactical plans for procurement, production, and shipment of the customer orders. Second, when done correctly, execution occurs per the detailed plans; there are linkage and coherence between the tactical planning and the specifics of what happens on the receiving dock, the plant floor, and the shipping dock.

We touched on MRP II earlier when we covered Demand Management in the chapter on customers. Let's now take a look at the total set of tools.

THE ELEMENTS OF MANUFACTURING RESOURCE PLANNING (MRP II)

Now it's time to look at all the pieces of Manufacturing Resource Planning, to see how they fit together. Figure 8-1 shows it graphically.

The top box in Figure 8-1, *Business Planning*, is not literally a part of MRP II; we show it in the diagram because it's a primary driver to all that follows. Business Planning generates the overall financial plans for the company: annual plans and budgets usually in monthly increments, plus longer-range plans in less detail typically covering a three- to five-year horizon. It's a projection of income and expenses for all major elements of the business and, as such, drives the budgeting process.

Business Planning, of course, is the responsibility of the top-management team: the president and his staff. Most companies do Business Planning very well.

Sales & Operations Planning (S&OP) addresses that part of the business plan that deals with sales, production, inventories, and backlog. In monthly increments, it's the tactical plan designed to execute the business plan. As such it's usually stated not in dollars, but rather in units of measure such as individual products, tons, gallons, standard hours, etc.

The Sales and Operations Plan is grouped into product families, broad categories of products of which there are typically a dozen or so per company. It establishes an aggregate plan of attack for Sales and Marketing, Product Development, Manufacturing, Purchasing, and Finance.

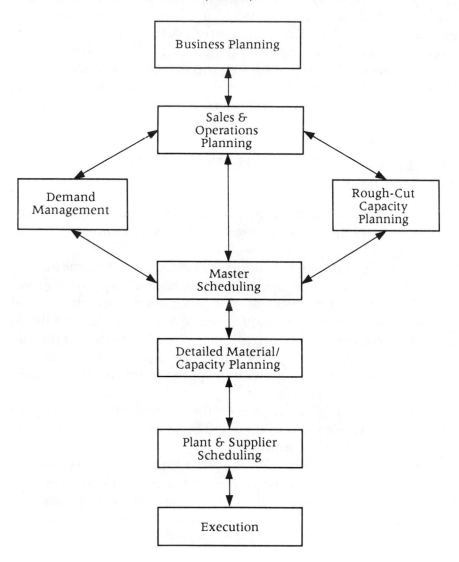

MANUFACTURING RESOURCE PLANNING
(MRP II)

FIGURE 8-1.

S&OP is primarily a tactical tool, but it has significant strategic overtones. As with Business Planning, the president and staff are responsible—and this is a very important factor. It has to do with linkage, and we'll return to it in later in this chapter.

Most companies do *not* do Sales and Operations Planning well. *Demand Management*, as we saw, has three major elements:

1. Effective sales forecasting, necessary in virtually all companies for resource acquisition and for financial planning.

2. Effective sales planning, the details of what Sales and Marketing have committed to sell and how they plan to do it. Involved here can be specific plans by individual, by territory, by product line, and by market channel.

3. Effective customer order entry and order promising, linked tightly to the manufacturing system.

Master Scheduling develops and maintains the anticipated build schedule for individual products. The master schedule is the detailed expression of the broader Sales and Operations plan; it specifies individual products (as opposed to families), and the time periods are weekly or smaller (as opposed to monthly). One key part of the master scheduler's job is to ensure that the sum of what's specified in the master schedule equals the Sales and Operations plan, as specified by top management. This creates a tight linkage between top management's plans and the detailed schedules that will drive specific activities in Sales, Manufacturing, and Purchasing.

Rough-Cut Capacity Planning is the process of converting the production side of the Sales and Operations plan—and the master schedule—into capacity needs for key resources: manpower, machinery, warehouse space, supplier capabilities, and in some cases money.

Money can be a significant constraint in a make-to-stock company with highly seasonal products. When I was in the sporting goods business, I learned that not many people buy baseballs in November. I also learned that we had to produce baseballs at a fairly level rate year-round, because the people who stitch the baseball covers are highly skilled and we couldn't afford to lose them via layoffs. This can present some serious cash-flow problems.

The objective with Rough-Cut Capacity Planning, therefore, is to apply a "sanity check" to determine whether or not the plans are attainable, and to provide direction regarding necessary changes in resources.

A brief digression. For most companies there's an enormous opportunity here for improved delivery performance. Today most manufacturing companies are operating some form of MRP/MRP II. Many of them, however, could do a far better job in these areas: Sales and Operations Planning, Demand Management, Master Scheduling, and Rough-Cut Capacity Planning. Those companies that do a good job find their ability to ship on time increases dramatically.

The next block, *Detailed Material/Capacity Planning*, actually contains two separate tools, similar in purpose but differing in mechanics:

1. Material Requirements Planning (MRP) translates the master schedule into requirements for the items needed to make the products. It does this via "exploding" the bill of material (formula, recipe) for the products into specific time-phased requirements for components and materials. In this process, it nets these requirements against inventories and open orders to determine the true needs for these items. It recommends actions such as releasing a new order or rescheduling orders already released. The logic of MRP is to drive matched sets of components into the finishing operations so that product can be put together and shipped.

2. Capacity Requirements Planning (CRP) is a tool used mainly by job shops (see next chapter). CRP takes the MRP plans for manufactured components and "translates" them into time-phased workload requirements for equipment and people. It compares these needs for capacity to the capacity that's available, and identifies those work centers where there is too little—or too much—capacity versus what's needed to meet the plan.

Moving down the diagram, we see *Plant & Supplier Scheduling.*

1. Plant Scheduling communicates the MRP-generated priorities to the people on the plant floor. For job shops, this is done via a technique called shop dispatching, which produces detailed priority lists. These spell out the relative priorities for each operation on every work order at all work centers.[1] For flow shops, the plant scheduling process often consists of fairly simple sequence lists (line schedules, cell schedules, process schedules) derived from MRP or the master schedule or, in some cases, from the customer orders themselves.

More and more, North American companies as well as Japanese use kanban to control production and material movement on the plant floor. In some cases it functions well on a stand-alone basis ("brand name" kanban); in situations with a high mix of items, it's typically used in conjunction with a schedule from the master scheduling function and/or MRP ("generic" kanban).

2. Supplier Scheduling (to be covered in Chapter 10) communicates the MRP plans for purchased items to their respective suppliers. This is typically done by supplier schedulers, within the framework of the business agreement (or contract) as negotiated by the buyers. Here also, the kanban technique can have major application. The supplier schedules communicate requirements through the medium to long term; kanban triggers the supplier for specific shipments.

The last box in the diagram is *Execution.* All that's gone before exists to make this possible, and this brings us to the important point that **SUPERIOR PLANNING ENABLES SUPERIOR EXECUTION.**

Now that we've seen the various components of this set of tools, we need to examine its overall characteristics.

MRP II ATTRIBUTES

Some important attributes of Manufacturing Resource Planning are shown in Figure 8-2. Let's look at each one.

Attributes of Manufacturing Resource Planning (MRP II)

- Internal linkage.
- Line accountability.
- Feedback.
- Financial integration.
- Simulation.
- Linkage with strategy.
- Integration with Just-in-Time.

FIGURE 8-2.

Internal Linkage

One of MRP II's most powerful contributions is its ability to translate the top-level plans made by the senior management group into valid short-term schedules for procurement, production, and shipment of the product to the customers.

We call this a "rack-and-pinion relationship." As high-level plans for product families change, MRP II gives people the ability to convert those changes—on a linked basis, with validity and coherence—into specific plans for products, components, materials, manpower, and machinery. This conversion is from macro to micro; from product families to products to specific components and ingredients, and from months to weeks to days and—in some cases—hours.

Line Accountability

The second principle concerns people. Not only are there linkage and coherence among the various levels of planning, there's also visibility. The people—those involved in both the execution and the planning—can see into the future plans. They can see what's expected of them in terms of shipments and production and procurement. In most cases, when MRP II is being operated correctly, they can see this early enough to make the necessary adjustments to meet the plan.

Feedback

The principle of "Silence is approval" applies here. It works this way: As long as you'll be able to meet the future plans in your area of responsibility, you don't need to say anything. However, when you see future planning calling for performance at a level beyond your current capacity, you must provide feedback to the next person up the line. Similarly, and of even more urgency, is when something goes wrong and you're unable to meet a plan which, until that moment, presented no problems. "Silence is approval" kicks in. You must then provide feedback to the next person up the line.

Manufacturing Resource Planning is people-focused and people-intensive. A common misunderstanding is that MRP II is a computer system.[2] It's not. It's a people system made possible by the computer.

Financial Integration

Manufacturing Resource Planning has the capability to integrate financial planning and control with the operating side of the business. Contained within MRP II are the sales plans, the production schedules for products and components, the schedules for delivery of materials from suppliers and subcontractors, manpower plans, speeds and feeds, and more. It's not a tough job to tie a dollar number onto each one of these elements.

Tactical plans and schedules—expressed in products, pieces, pounds, gallons, hours, etc.—can be translated into a different unit of measurement: dollars. With MRP II it becomes a practical matter to derive profit pro formas, cash-flow projections, product costs, inventory valuations, variance reporting, and budgets directly from those operating numbers.

Simulation

Simulation provides the capability to ask "what-if" questions and to receive understandable, actionable answers. Spread-sheet software gives one the ability to vary one factor in an array and see the effect of that upon other elements.[3] Well, the MRP II data base can serve as a "giant spread sheet." It enables people to answer questions like these:

- Can we accept this customer order and ship it when the customer is asking for it? Do we have enough material and capacity to do it?

- If not, can we use material and capacity allocated to make-to-stock products? Will doing that cause those products to go on back order, and if so, for how long?

- Alternatively, can we take material and capacity allocated to other customer orders? If so, which customers will be affected and how long will their orders be delayed?

Or another scenario:

We're hearing rumors that the competition is working on a new product similar to the one we're developing. We want to beat them to the market.

To ensure that, we want to move up the new product launch by ninety days. Do we have the capacity in Plant 1 to do that? If not, can some of Plant 1's work be off-loaded to Plant 3?

Which are the critical purchased materials? Are there any major subcontracting steps involved? It won't do us any good to have enough capacity in our own plants if our suppliers don't have enough in theirs.

Here's another point on simulation, and it's an important one: Since MRP II can be expressed in dollars as well as units, the simulations can also be done in financial terms. The operational simulation helps people answer the question "Can we do it? Can we pull up the new product launch by ninety days?" If the answer to that question is yes, then the proposed plan can be run in financial terms, to help answer the question "Do we really want to do it? What will be the impact on the bottom line? How will cash flow be affected?"

When the decisions are made, the people can enter the necessary changes into their current planning and proceed to execute accordingly. Simulation is a very important aspect of Manufacturing Resource Planning, one of its most powerful features.

Linkage with Strategy

Let's return to the issue of linkage. Strategic planning and tactical planning are linked together. But how? The answer to that question is shown in Figure 8-3.

Here's another case where the whole is greater than the sum of its parts. Companies must not only excel in strategic and tactical planning, they must also link the two processes together. Companies that do this, over the long run, will be able to consistently "out-execute" their competitors.

Let's take a look at a chemical company that's made great strides using the tools of Manufacturing Resource Planning.

Excellence in Action: PYOSA, Monterrey, Mexico[4]

PYOSA is a major manufacturer of pigments, dyes, lead oxides, agrochemicals, and ceramics. It has five divisions producing products for customers in Mexico, the U.S., Central and South America, and the Far East.

In 1986, PYOSA was faced with increased foreign competition, substantial operating inefficiencies, and burgeoning inventories of raw materials and finished goods. In an attempt to improve their financial picture, they slashed inventories. Care to guess what happened to delivery performance? Right, it plummeted. Once again, the inventory-versus-delivery trade-off reared its ugly head.

Instead of bemoaning their fate, the people at PYOSA decided to make that trade-off go away. And the technology they selected was Manufacturing Resource Planning.

In so doing, they ignored the conventional wisdom of the time that MRP II doesn't apply to process companies. They didn't say, "We're unique; we're different; this won't work for us." Instead they said, "We can make this work." And they did, with a vengeance.

What followed was one of the best implementations I've ever seen, the equal of any in the United States and better than most. All five divisions of PYOSA implemented MRP II in less than two and a half years, and reached the Class A performance level a few months later.

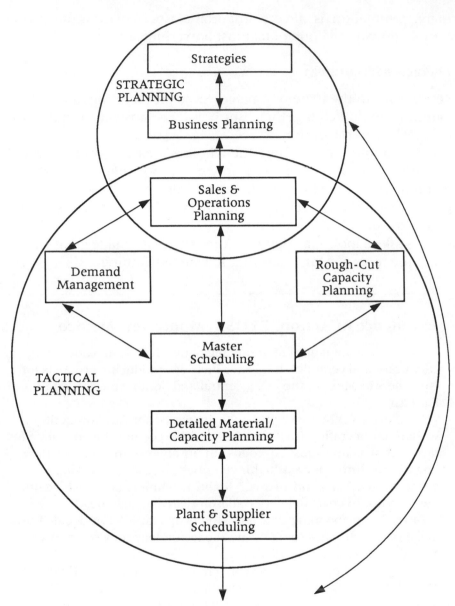

FIGURE 8-3.

Results? Inventory's down a third, but look what's happened to delivery performance. Here's Rubén Sáez, Director of the Pigments Division: "A year ago our customer service was, at best, 50 percent. Now our fill rate is 95 percent. Customers who said horrible things about us before now think we're terrific, and it's showing up in our increased market share!"

Sáez goes on to say: "[MRP II] is the only tool that gives the ability to change the future. It's the only way people can look into the future and communicate and make things happen. They can react ahead of time rather than when it's too late."

Customers now have faith in PYOSA, and many have reduced their own inventories, because they can depend on PYOSA to ship on time. A number of them are sharing their future planning information with PYOSA, thereby reducing the need to forecast.

Eduardo Rodriguez, Unit Production Manager, puts it this way: "We used to say that only a wizard could predict what was going to happen tomorrow, let alone next week. Sales forecasts used to change every two hours—now we have two weeks' lead time. We can even look three to four months ahead and predict . . . where we will be and what we will need. We work with the customers to forecast what they are likely to need and educate them on our system so they have a better idea of what we're doing. We show them that with better forecasts, they are controlling their own destiny in making sure they have what they need when they need it."

How about flexibility? Plant superintendent Gabriel Santoy changed his views about what the plant needed: "I originally thought we wanted a stable schedule from week to week. Now that we have MRP II in place, I can manage a vastly changing schedule—one that matches the real world. The market is not constant, so our plant must be flexible. Now we have the ability to do that."

Let's not overlook cost efficiency. Here's one last quote, this one from Alberto Fernández, the CEO: "MRP II is the end link in a chain of events, the culmination of everyone working together. Now that we are functioning better as a team, we have to focus on becoming more competitive worldwide. Our government just opened our borders last year to free trade, so we now have to compete in an international market. To do that, we must become as efficient as possible. That's something that never stops."

Manufacturing Resource Planning enables a company to do the basics extremely well: ship on time, reduce inventories, become more flexible. But because it forces a company to get control over its operations, it's more than that. If you're out of control, it's hard to be excellent at Total Quality Control, or Just-in-Time, or to get much bang for the buck from automation. MRP II can be an important foundation element, serving as the launch pad for future improvement initiatives.

Back in the 1960s, Black and Decker became one of the first successful MRP users. Their reason: They wanted to be able to do the routine things routinely, so that they would have time to do the extraordinary things. Shipping product on time needs to be a routine thing; holding the retail prices of power tools virtually constant, in *current* dollars, over a thirty-year period containing high inflation is an extraordinary thing.

MRP II's Integration with Just-in-Time

TRADE-OFF ALERT: Back in the mid-1980s, there raged a fierce debate between the JIT enthusiasts ("jitters") and the MRP II believers ("merpers"). The jitters claimed that MRP II was no longer necessary; the merpers stated that JIT as a planning tool was inferior. This created much confusion. People wondered if they went to JIT would they need to give up MRP II—or vice versa. Should we do JIT, or should we do MRP II?

The answer now is very clear: You need to intelligently use both. Here's an example, which I picked up in a conversation with an ex-Hewlett-Packard employee. She was talking about their Just-in-Time transition from a job shop to a flow shop. At one point, she told me, they had more people entering data into their shop floor control and labor reporting system than making the parts!

Well, rest assured that situation didn't last long. Did they throw out all of MRP II? Definitely not. But they did drop their conventional shop floor control system and replaced it with something much simpler.

Does that mean that they were no longer "doing MRP II?" Not at all. They were doing it better than ever. As Just-in-Time guided them to simplify the environment, the planning and control tools of MRP II could be simplified also.

We can now describe the relationship of Manufacturing Resource Planning and Just-in-Time as follows:

- Manufacturing Resource Planning is a set of tools for planning and scheduling. It enables a company to maximize its performance out of today's operating environment.

- Just-in-Time is a focused attack on waste. It forces constant improvements to today's environment so that tomorrow's environment will be better.

- Manufacturing Resource Planning then enables a company to maximize performance out of tomorrow's improved environment.

- While that's going on, Just-in-Time is hard at work making improvements to tomorrow's environment, so that next week's environment will be better than tomorrow's.

- When next week comes, MRP II will be there to maximize performance out of that environment.

- And on and on and on.

MRP II will not remain static during this process. It will almost invariably become simpler—because the operating environment has become simpler thanks to Just-in-Time. Hewlett-Packard's experience is the rule, not the exception.

These two very powerful tools are mutually supportive. Just-in-Time enables Manufacturing Resource Planning to become simpler and easier to operate. MRP II allows a company to get the maximum mileage out of the improvements that Just-in-Time has generated. Most successful users of Just-in-Time are also successful users of MRP II.

STRATEGIC CHECKUP

- Is there a formal process within the company for Sales and Operations Planning, so that top-level decisions can be made on a focused, rigorous, and timely basis?

- Are the Sales and Marketing departments pro-actively involved in this process?

- Is there a rack-and-pinion relationship between these high-level decisions and what happens in Customer Service, Production, and Purchasing?

- Is the business being run with only one set of numbers? Are the financials derived directly from the operating data being used to run the business on a day-to-day basis?

In the next chapter, we'll look at one part of the company's infrastructure: its facilities and equipment.

CHAPTER NINE

Facilities and Equipment—
The Muscle and Bone, Part I

"The healthy, competitive company understands the need to nurture, not neglect, these important elements. . . . [It] 'takes care of itself' and stays fit and trim."

A few years ago I heard an angry general manager tell his manufacturing vice president to start talking English and stop talking alphabet soup. He'd had too much of FMS's, AGV's, CNC's, and other arcane acronyms.

This isn't uncommon. "Old school" manufacturing people often resorted to this approach in self-defense. They did it to help deflect some of the arrows coming their way for not having perfect quality, or perfect deliveries, or total flexibility, or low cost—or all of the above.

Sometimes it worked. Sometimes it worked for many years. But it shouldn't be that way, for two reasons. First, working as a team with purpose, the top management group can lead an effective drive toward zero trade-offs. Second, the manufacturing side of the business is inherently no more complex than Marketing, Finance, Legal, or Product Design. Manufacturing is mostly common sense, applied to some basic concepts. A design engineering manager from Boeing attended one of our seminars several years ago. About halfway through the session, he said to me, "This isn't rocket science, is it?" I laughed and said, "No, John, it sure isn't. It's basic blocking and tackling, organized common sense."

Let's take a look at the important issues here—plant location, focus, flow, automation, capacity strategies, and some issues involving capital budgeting—and see if they can't be "de-complicated" somewhat.

PLANT LOCATION/RELOCATION

This is less of a hot topic today than it was ten or twenty years ago, for several reasons.

First, new brick and mortar is not as necessary today. Thanks to tools like Just-in-Time, Total Quality Control, Manufacturing Resource Planning, and others, many companies are now producing substantially more volume out of the same square feet of plant floor space. Often these improvements in space utilization go far beyond increases of 10 or 30 or 50 percent; they are order of magnitude increases—two, three, four, or more times. More and more, I find myself pointing out to people that the road to operational excellence is littered with white elephants.

By white elephants, I mean:

- The unused warehouses and stockrooms that used to be filled with raw material and finished inventory no longer needed.

- The empty plant floor space that held work-in-process inventories and/or equipment that have been eliminated. In many cases, happily, the freed-up plant and warehouse space has been converted into offices to hold, for example, expanded engineering staffs required to support new products—or for other uses such as cafeterias and recreation areas.

- The new plants that were authorized but never finished, justified rationally on historical data but no longer necessary in the light of dramatically enhanced efficiency.

The message: Look to the future, not the past, when evaluating the need for expansion of your physical plant. More brick and mortar may not be needed. In many cases, it will not be needed if you're on a continuous improvement track.

There's a second reason for less attention being paid to the plant location issue today: The rush to locate plants in areas of low labor cost—often offshore—has subsided. A sharp drop in the direct labor component of many companies' products, thanks to tools mentioned above, plus automation and others, has contributed to this trend. Further, particularly as it relates to relocating plants offshore, there is a growing awareness that savings in direct labor can be more than offset by extra freight and inventory costs, loss of flexibility, increased lead times, and attendant poor delivery performance.

Last and certainly not least is the people issue. Many companies are improving their ability to educate, involve, and empower their people. As the work force develops into teams of self-directed, problem-solving innovators, people become not only partners, but an enormously valuable asset. Losing them for the sake of a plant relocation becomes unthinkable. One more time: The issue is how to *maximize labor's value*, not minimize its cost.

Given all of the above, however, the need does arise from time to time for decisions regarding plant location. The "standard" criteria are well known: proximity to customers, suppliers, work force, natural resources, transportation infrastructure, and so forth. In addition to those, however, the following questions need to be addressed:

1. Will the location under consideration support, or will it be counter to, the customer-driven strategy? This is the overriding test, the ultimate "hurdle rate."

2. As a corollary to number 1, specifically how will this location enable the company to serve its customers better?

3. Another corollary to number 1, what's the people impact of this location decision? Is this an area with good quality of life? Will it enhance, or degrade, the company's ability to attract and retain superior people?

FOCUS

Focus is a simple concept, but a very powerful one.

A plant that makes relatively few products, serving one or only a few markets, is said to be focused. The plant with many products, processes, and/or markets is considered to be complex. Complexity is bad; simplicity is good and very important.

According to Wickham Skinner, a focused facility

> can become a competitive weapon because its entire apparatus is focused to accomplish the particular manufacturing task demanded by the company's overall strategy and marketing objective. . . . The conventional factory produces many products for numerous customers in a variety of markets, thereby demanding the performance of a multiplicity of manufacturing tasks all at once from one set of assets *and people.* [Emphasis added.] Its rationale is "economy of scale" and lower capital investment.
>
> However the result more often than not is a hodge-podge of compromises, a high overhead, and a manufacturing organization that is constantly in hot water with top management, marketing management, the controller, and customers.[1]

To this day, in North America, we still have far fewer focused plants than otherwise. Why? Maybe because nonfocused (read "complex") is the easy way out.

Let's say that a company has just developed a new product. They'll have to decide where to produce it. Which of the following two approaches will require less time, effort, dialogue, mental energy, etc.?

1. They can "dump it into an existing plant."

2. They can determine the operational strategy for the new product in order to best support the marketing strategy and win orders in the marketplace. They need to define Manufacturing's key objectives for this product and then do a match-up with the explicit strategic priorities for existing products. (If these explicit, well-defined strategies don't exist, of course

they'll have to develop them.) They then make their decision based on this analysis.

Which of these two approaches is easier? The first, obviously, and that's the way it's been done time and time again. But this is not the route to success. Taking the first approach may cause the plant to deal with a set of objectives, requirements, and problems for the new product that are very different from the existing product(s) it produces. The result may well be the hodge-podge of compromises, confusion, and sub-par performance cited earlier. And the situation will get worse, not better, as more dissimilar products are dumped into the plant. The best method is focus-driven. That's the way it's done in leading-edge companies in the U.S., Japan, and Europe.

Does this mean that you have to build a new plant for each new product? Not at all. If you have room in an existing plant, use your existing capacity through focused manufacturing.

Create what's called a "plant-within-a-plant." Doing this involves setting up separate organizations within the plant for various product lines. Each unit is then able to structure its resources (people, equipment, systems) for the very best fit to accomplish the task at hand. They can mobilize intensely to support the strategic thrust of that part of the company and to enhance its competitive posture.

Increasingly, we're seeing winning companies operate on the basis that **THERE IS MORE TO BE GAINED COMPETITIVELY FROM FOCUSED FACILITIES THAN FROM ECONOMY OF SCALE.**

A focused facility, whether a separate plant or a plant-within-a-plant, will probably be smaller than its nonfocused counterpart. Is this bad? I don't think so. In fact, I think it's good, in almost all cases.

There are companies that have, as a stated part of their operational strategy, established an upper limit on plant size; they don't want any unit to become larger than X hundred employees. When that limit is approached, they split off another plant or business unit—sometimes in the same building, often on the same grounds or in the same geographic area.

Is there a universal target, an upper limit, for the number of people in a plant? Not really. In some industries—automobiles, steel, and shipbuilding come to mind—larger facilities are necessary for reasons of scale economies. The average auto plant will have more people than the average electronics plant, for example, or pharmaceuticals plant. The important point, however, is that the average plant in most industries is smaller today than a few years ago. There is a very visible trend in North America to "de-massify" manufacturing (and often other parts of the organization as well).

Ron Brookbank, formerly President of the Association for Manufacturing Excellence, cited the importance of "smallness." He feels that improvement initiatives have the best chance of success when they enable employees to rally around something—such as a particular product line or a plant unit—and establish a commonality of mission. Brookbank said, "Within large entities, it is difficult to get employee empowerment. But when you begin to break it down and focus on common objectives [within a cohesive group], you start to get results."[2]

Small *is* beautiful when dealing with people, and that's what plants are mostly about—people.

Well, if plants are mostly about people, doesn't it follow that the issue of plant focus is largely about people? It is indeed.[3] When focusing or creating plants-within-a-plant, the primary issue is people and how they'll be organized. How the equipment is laid out is an important but secondary issue. One could make a good case that this discussion of plant focus belongs more appropriately in the chapter on people rather than in this one, but it's here because it fits so closely with our next topic: flow.

Companies are focusing not only within Manufacturing, but also beyond. People from both manufacturing and nonmanufacturing areas are being integrated into operational units focused by customer group and/or product. The primary goal is to enable the people inside the company to get closer to the people outside the company who buy the product: to better serve them with faster deliveries and with products that meet and exceed their expectations. Here's a superb example.

Excellence in Action:

RADIO CAP COMPANY, SAN ANTONIO, TEXAS

Radio Cap produces advertising specialty products—custom-imprinted caps, mugs, and beverage holders. They produce around 100,000 customer orders per year.

The company's recent drive to operational excellence centered around a simultaneous implementation of Manufacturing Resource Planning and Just-in-Time, and a key part of that has been "to create separate sets of operations for each major product line. In effect, each set of operations . . . constitutes a 'mini-factory' in which customer orders enter at one end and finished product pops out the other."[4]

Because much of the work on a customer order used to take place before the order ever hit the plant floor, Radio Cap extended its focused units from "the front door through to the shipping dock." People in a single unit include: order-entry people, customer service representatives, artists, typesetters, prep people, production associates—everyone it takes to get an order out the door.

Today Radio Cap ships customer orders in five days, versus an industry average of twenty. As a result, sales have increased from $15 million to $25 million in two years, and are projected to go to $50 million within the next four.

They're working hard at getting that five-day shipment cycle down to four, then three, then two—and then to hours. One of their executives pointed out: "The day is coming where our orders will be so quick and happen so reliably that our customers will stop calling to inquire about the status of an order, because they'll already have the product. We're going to create a market that wasn't there before. . . ."

Process Focus?

Thus far we've talked about focusing by customer and/or product. I believe that by far this is the best approach.

Some people talk about a *process* focus, where perhaps one plant would do all the preliminary fabrication, another the component finishing, another the subassembly work, and yet another the final assembly.

Admittedly, there are some industries where a process focus may be mandatory because of the nature of the processes, safety and health issues, the enormous capital investment required, and/or other reasons. However, as a general rule, talk about a process focus makes me nervous. Part of the problem with U.S. industry is that it has been far too focused on production processes and has largely ignored customers.

These are the 1990s—the era of customer service, customer satisfaction, customer linking, and exceeding customer requirements. The excellent companies—the ones that win—will continually delight their customers. Focusing organizations and equipment on products and/or customers, rather than on manufacturing processes, is the best way to get there.

Now let's look at another important issue, flow, because it ties right in with focus.

FLOW

There are, broadly, two basic approaches to how companies arrange their facilities: job shop and flow shop. Other terms you may have come across—batch, intermittent, connected versus disconnected flow—are essentially subsets of either job shop or flow. We don't need to concern ourselves with them here.

Job Shop

First, let's define job shop. Many people feel that a job shop is "a place where you make specials." Well, it's true that specials can be made in a job shop, but so can standard products.

Some people think that job shops are small places with a few dozen people and lots of different equipment. Yes, they can be that, but they can also be much larger. McDonnell-Douglas of Canada used to have over fifteen hundred people working in their job shop (prior to a major reorganization into more focused manufacturing units). What constitutes a job shop is not size, nor making specials. The issue is how the resources are organized.

Let's try this definition on for size: A job shop is a form of manufacturing organization where the resources are grouped by like type. Some call it a "functional" form of organization; others, "single-function departments."

The classic example of this approach is a machine shop. Here all the lathes are in one area, the drill presses in another, the milling machines in another, and the automatic screw machines are in the building next door.[5] In a job shop, the work moves from work center to work center based on routings unique to the individual items being produced. In some job shops, there can be dozens, or even hundreds, of different operations within a single routing.

Do job shops exist in companies other than metalworking? You bet. I can remember one from my years in the pharmaceutical industry, specifically that part of the plant where we made tablets and capsules. We had a granulating department, a compressing department, a coating department, a capsule-filling department, etc. The nature of the product would determine its routing. Tablets got compressed; capsules didn't. Some tablets got coated; some didn't. Capsules got filled but didn't get compressed.

This is a job shop, by the above definition. And please note: At the pharmaceutical plant, we didn't make "specials." We made the same products, to the same specifications, time and time again. The Food and Drug Administration prefers it that way.

Advantages typically attributed to the job shop form of organization include a higher rate of equipment utilization and enhanced flexibility.

Flow Shop

This a form of manufacturing organization where the resources are grouped by their sequence in the process. Some refer to it as a "process" layout; others, "in-line."

Examples include oil refineries, certain chemical manufacturing operations, an automobile assembly line, a filling line in a consumer package goods plant, or a manufacturing cell.

Back to the pharmaceutical company, making tablets and capsules. The filling and packaging operation was flow, not job shop. Each work center (line) consisted of some very dissimilar pieces of equipment in a very precise sequence: a bottle cleaner, a filler, a cotton stuffer, a capper, a labeler, a case packer, etc. Note: We didn't have all of the cotton stuffers over in one corner of the department, as the job shop layout would call for. This would have been very slow, inefficient, wasteful of space, etc.

In most situations in most companies, flow is far superior to job shop:

- Products can be made faster, with shorter lead times and a greater responsiveness to customers' needs.

- Inventories, both work-in-process and other, are smaller. Less space is required; fewer dollars are tied up; obsolescence is less likely.

- Less material handling is required. Non-value-adding activities are reduced with an attendant rise in productivity and reduced risk of damage.

- People are better able to identify with the product. And the result is more involvement, higher morale, and better ideas for improvement.

There are other benefits from flow, one of which is simplicity. See Figure 9-1.

Which is simpler, job shop or flow shop? Which is easier to understand? Which is less difficult to plan and schedule? Which allows for more visual control and more immediate feedback? The obvious answer, and the correct one, to all of these questions is flow shop.

Well, so what? Unless you're fully a flow shop today, what should you do? The answer is, wherever possible, you should be converting to flow. If you don't, and your competition has a flow operation, you might be in deep trouble. And your competitors may be doing just that, because there is a significant movement worldwide to flow manufacturing. Harley-Davidson is living testi-

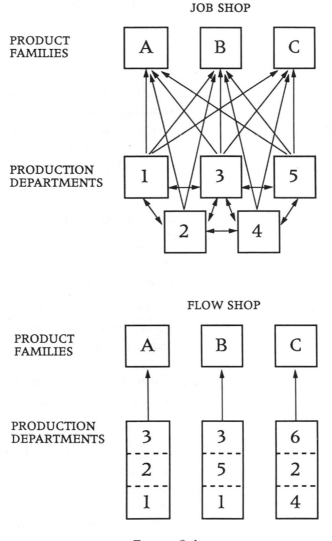

FIGURE 9-1.

mony to the benefits of a flow operation. Of all the many good things Harley people did following their buy-out from AMF, one of the most important is that they got very serious about Just-in-Time. Much of their JIT progress centered around the creation of flow manufacturing. In some cases they were able to create flow without even moving the equipment, by dedicating certain machines to certain tasks.

Cellular Manufacturing

So how did Harley and others convert from job shop to flow? Answer: They used cellular manufacturing. Companies are migrating from job shop to flow via the creation of manufacturing cells (also called flow lines, demand pull lines, kanban lines, and probably some other terms that are just now being dreamed up).

Here's how many companies do it.

1. The industrial engineers do a Pareto analysis on the most common routes of manufacture through the shop.

2. They select a given routing, which may cover only 1 or 2 percent of the items but account for 5 or 10 percent of the plant throughput.

3. They pull various pieces of equipment from the job shop and place them in an adjacent sequence per the routing.

See Figure 9-2, the top part of which is a simplified schematic of a job shop. As such it shows all similar machines grouped together.

The bottom part of Figure 9-2 shows what the cell would look like after its creation. Note how very different pieces of equipment, and their operators, are now located side by side.

A job shop has just been converted to flow. Material goes into the front end of the cell, and finished products (or parts) come out the back end. When this occurs, all of the benefits cited above can be realized.

What happens next? What should *not* happen next is *nothing*. What *should* happen next is to go back to Step 1, run another Pareto on the items still remaining in the job shop, and create the second cell.

And then do it again. And again. And again. The folks at Tektronix have a saying: "Never stop celling." On the other coast, Black and Decker's superb plant at Tarboro, North Carolina, also

JOB SHOP

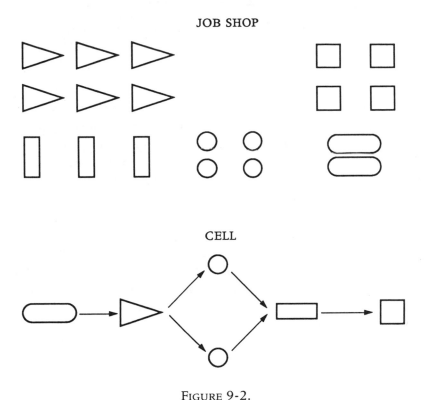

CELL

FIGURE 9-2.

has had great success with cells. In their power cord production operation, lead times have gone from days (job shop) to minutes (cell), work-in-process inventory is virtually zero, and thousands of square feet of space have been freed up.

Here's Clarence Bauer, at the time department manager in charge of power cord production at Tarboro: "After we completed this, we kept asking why in the world didn't we do it this way before? It makes absolutely no sense to have done it any other way."[6]

And they did this for virtually no money; their only expenditure was the man-hours spent to move the equipment into the cell. How's that for low cost and quick payback?

Does it always happen that way, creating cells for no money? Of course not. Sometimes new equipment's necessary and that might be the bad news. Here's the good news:

1. Often the new equipment required for the cell can be simple, single-purpose, lower-cost machinery as opposed to the more expensive, general-purpose gear that's often purchased to go into the job shop.

2. The benefits are substantial. Ask yourselves what it's worth to wipe out big hunks of inventory, free up floor space, and dramatically shorten your lead times to your customers. Ask yourselves: "What should we do with our money? Keep it tied up in inventory? Or put some of it into better equipment and put the rest into the R&D, or Marketing, or the bank?"

Can companies eliminate all of their job shop as they move to flow? Sometimes yes; often no. In most cases, though they can produce a very high percentage of their throughput via flow, and do the low-volume orders in the remaining job shop. Pareto's Law really works in our favor here.

THE FOCUS-FLOW CONNECTION

Focus and flow go together. They're mutually reinforcing, highly supportive of each other. Focus provides the strategic framework for macro plant decisions. This concept should be the driver for the overall organization of people, plant, and equipment.

Flow, on the other hand, has a more detailed aspect to it. It's the driver for the specifics of facility organization, at a given plant or a given plant-within-a-plant, as defined by the need to focus. As such, flow is conceptually subordinated to focus. However, in many cases, flow makes it easier to focus and/or makes possible a higher degree of focus. Flow "disentangles" production resources from a functional, departmental, job shop organization to one more focused on the product.

Traditional thinking in the field of manufacturing strategy has often centered around the relative merits of job shop versus flow. The issue of which to choose was traditionally presented as a major strategic decision.

I don't agree with that. I don't think that's appropriate any longer. The overwhelming advantages of flow and cellular manu-facturing have been proven time and time again.

Sure, there may be a few companies around with so few com-mon items and processes that no flow is possible, but such com-panies are really few and far between.[7] Virtually all companies can make use of flow to one degree or another. Here's how it might break out:

1. Minor opportunity for flow. "We're totally 'design-to-order.' We never make the same product twice. However, we do make the same *types* of product repeatedly. Within those families there are some common components, and we can create cells to manufacture those."

2. Major opportunity for flow. "What are we waiting for? That guy from Black and Decker hit the nail on the head. It doesn't make any sense not to go to flow."

3. Already there. "What's all the excitement about? We've been doing it this way for years. We make chemicals [or consumer package goods or containers]."

The issue isn't whether or not you should flow. The only issue is: how much. And you don't need to predetermine that. Just get started. Never stop celling.

AUTOMATION

In this category we find things like robots, flexible manufacturing systems (FMS), automated guided vehicles (AGV), automated storage/retrieval systems (AS/RS), and automated test equipment. All of these are excellent tools, although, some would argue, AS/RS's shouldn't be widely needed in this age of Just-in-Time.

One problem with automation is that some companies have pursued it as an end in itself. They had, one could say, a strategy to automate, rather than a strategy to establish close customer link-ages and to enhance their people's ability to serve those customers. As a result, automation's received bad press.

One example is my "alma mater," General Motors, which as we

said earlier pumped billions of dollars into factory automation during the 1980s. In so doing, they raised their break-even point instead of lowering it. At the same time, Toyota was leading the GM/Toyota joint venture in Fremont, California (NUMMI), to be the most productive plant in GM—without heavy automation.

Automation for its own sake is not a good idea. Rather, automation should follow prior efforts toward simplification and continuous improvement like setup reduction, cells, source assurance of quality, and many of the other good things we saw in the chapter on continuous improvement.

Reasons frequently given to automate—ones that make sense to me—include the following:

1. To shorten lead times, thereby getting closer to the customer.

2. To remove people from hazardous jobs.

3. To remove people from boring jobs.

4. To reduce the variability of a process, thereby raising quality.

5. To enable further cost reductions, on top of substantial progress already made through simplification and continuous improvement processes.

Many winning companies have adopted the following: **PLANT AUTOMATION IS NOT AN END, ONLY A MEANS, TO HELP THE COMPANY'S PEOPLE BETTER SERVE THEIR CUSTOMERS.**

Before you sign up for a big-dollar automation project, apply this principle, and the above criteria, against it. If it fits, then consider going forward with the automation. If not, forget it and spend that time out on the plant floor talking with the world's leading experts about what they need to do their jobs better.

COMPUTER INTEGRATED MANUFACTURING (CIM)

A great deal has been written about Computer Integrated Manufacturing during the past decade or so. The bad news is that most people aren't really sure what it is. Ask ten people for a definition of CIM and you'll get close to ten different answers.

In the narrow sense, it refers to tying together the "islands of automation" on the plant floor, via electronic linkages. It is heavily process-control oriented. That's fine, but in the larger scheme of things, it's not a terribly high-priority item—not enough to get excited about unless you happen to be writing ad copy for a CIM hardware or software supplier.

The broader and more important meaning of Computer Integrated Manufacturing is "the integration of all information (engineering, business, and process control) involved in the total spectrum of manufacturing activity."[8] As such, it's an emerging technology; it'll take some time before its use is widespread.

Here are several points to keep in mind if you're considering CIM:

- CIM should be evaluated like any other improvement initiative. First and foremost is the question "How will this help us increase customer satisfaction?"

- CIM does not meet the criteria we've defined for highly attractive projects. First, it's not low cost. Second, it'll take quite a while to pay back. Third, some would argue that it's not completely proven.

- Beware of an excessive focus on the C item (the computer—as in "computer integrated manufacturing"). The true priority is to support the A item (the people).

Certainly we'll see much more functional integration over the next ten years, and much of that will be computer supported. In fact, it's already happening; companies that implement effective Manufacturing Resource Planning find that MRPII has a highly integrating effect among Sales, Marketing, Finance, Product Development, and Manufacturing: accurate and comprehensive data, one set of numbers, everyone "singing off the same sheet of music." To the extent that CIM can enhance this, it'll be a winner.

CAPACITY STRATEGY

The issue of capacity plays a major role regarding facilities, so we certainly need to get this topic on the table. First, let's recognize that there are four major dimensions to capacity changes:

1. *Direction*. Do we need to increase capacity or decrease capacity? With few exceptions, the answer here is obvious; it's unlikely that a company will think it needs to increase capacity when it has too much, and vice versa. Let's move on, focusing on capacity increases.

2. *Bottleneck*. Which is the constraining resource? Are there more than one? How much more capacity will be needed in the bottleneck? Answers here can usually be obtained from effective capacity-planning techniques that do not require a scientist, rocket or otherwise. We'll cover them in the next section.

3. *Size*. In what size does the capacity increase come, small increments or large? If small, it's usually not a high dollar issue (relative to total demand) and therefore easier to deal with than capacity that can be obtained only in large "chunks." Adding another wave solder machine for an electronics facility, for example, can be an easier issue to deal with than building an entire chemical plant.

4. *Timing*. From a strategic standpoint, this is the most important of the four capacity factors and deserves the most attention. Let's take a closer look.

Lead Versus Lag

The timing issue breaks out broadly into two choices: lag or lead. A lag strategy says to lag the market, to hold off on capacity increases until the higher level of demand is present. Once the market demand is there, then get more capacity.

A lead strategy says to lead the market, to get the additional capacity *in advance of* the increase in market demand. Then, as the demand picks up, the company will be ready to service it.

Either option has a clear downside. To follow a lead strategy means you'll incur the costs of the additional capacity before the higher demand kicks in. Further, there is the risk that the market won't develop as forecasted. In that case, the costs of the extra capacity will be around for some time, until it can be sold or converted to other uses.

On the other hand, the lag strategy can be costly—perhaps even more so. Included here would be the "scramble" costs of overtime, expediting, confusion, and others. Most companies will incur these costs, because they will scramble like mad to service as much of the higher demand as possible out of the existing facilities and work force. A lag strategy is almost always implicit. It's not spelled out anywhere; it just happens.

As the company scrambles, another cost often rears its ugly head: the cost of unhappy customers. With tongue in cheek, I'll point out that customers can be a pain in the neck. They can be really picky. For some strange reason customers don't like back orders, late deliveries, long lead times, and—oh, yes—poor quality. And yet a lag strategy coupled with a scramble mentality will frequently result in those very things. The resulting costs may never show up specifically in the accounting records, but they can be enormous.

Bottom line: Achieving *and maintaining* true operational excellence is more difficult with a lag strategy. It can be done, but it requires enormous organizational self-discipline. It means the company must be truthful to the customers—to turn away their orders in excess of current capacity and/or to promise those orders for delivery further in the future than the customers want. (To minimize the pain of stretched-out lead times, some companies allocate capacity for preferred customers, thereby retaining their ability to ship quickly to them.)

TRADE-OFF ALERT: The ability to "flex" capacity—to ramp up and down effectively and economically—can help reduce the pressure on this lead/lag issue. In the perfect world, a company would have 100 percent flexibility for capacity increases up or down at no penalty in quality, delivery, cost, continuity of employment, etc. The issue of lead-versus-lag capacity would naturally go away.

But the world's not perfect, and this issue will always be present. The challenge is to mute it—to make it a less critical issue—via flexibility. Traditional ways to do this include overtime, the use of temporary employees, and subcontracting—and these are fine as long as quality, delivery, cost, and so forth aren't negatively impacted.

Additionally, some of the technologies and tools we've covered earlier can be employed to solve this problem. Skill Based Pay (to help the work force become more flexible) and Cellular Manufacturing (to free up space, thus eliminating or at least postponing the need for more brick and mortar) are two that come to mind. As the company becomes increasingly flexible, the "band width" of volume within which it can operate well becomes broader.

Good planning tools also play an important role here. Let's take a look.

Capacity Planning

Effective capacity-planning tools can help a great deal, regardless of which capacity strategy the company is pursuing. For those with a lead strategy, good capacity planning gives advance warning of future bottlenecks so that decisions can be made on a rigorous, focused basis, leading to early action to acquire the needed capacity.

With a lag strategy, effective capacity planning—working in concert with rigorous demand management and a well-managed master schedule—enables a company to promise customer orders with integrity. The same capacity is not promised to two different customers, and orders will continue to ship on time. Quoted lead times will be extended, of course, as they book more orders per unit of time than can be produced. Their customers will be told of the new schedule in advance of planning the order. The customers can then make an informed decision to live with the longer delivery times or to go elsewhere.

Do some companies actually follow this approach? You bet they do, and more than one might think. Even companies with lead strategies get surprised with business far above forecast. Being honest with the customers, building trust, and nurturing customer/supplier relationships are far more important to these excellent companies.

CAPITAL BUDGETING

It's no secret that many operating executives in North America are not enthusiastic about their corporation's ground rules for justifying expenditures for new plants and equipment. Frequently cited are an overemphasis on financial measures, such as hurdle rates for investment payback, and an underemphasis on nonfinancial elements such as quality, flexibility, safety, morale, and what the competition's up to.

Yes, it's a problem. And it's based on an incorrect view of the world, depicted in Figure 9-3.

This assumes that if the investment is not made, things will continue as before. And that can be a very shaky assumption, because the competition may not be sitting still. The more likely scenario is shown in Figure 9-4.

In the medium to long run, the riskiest option is to do nothing—don't invest, don't change, don't improve. You can run but you can't hide. The competitive world is not standing still.

Clinging to the status quo is a high-risk, not a no-risk, strategy. It can be a fatal option. As with free lunches, there is no such thing as

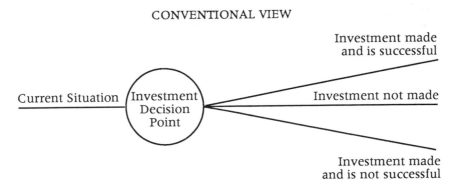

FIGURE 9-3.

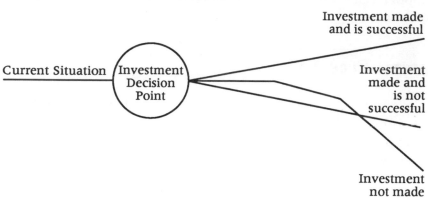

FIGURE 9-4.

a no-risk strategy. Companies must change. The issue is "Who controls the change, you or your competition?"

STRATEGIC CHECKUP

- Are there advantages to be gained in the company by increased focus of facilities, equipment, and organization—both within and outside of Manufacturing?

- Is the company taking full advantage of flow manufacturing?

- Is plant automation pursued primarily as a means to help the company's people better serve their customers?

- Does the company have a formal capacity strategy—to lead or to lag?

- Do the company's capital budgeting procedures assume the maintenance of the status quo?

Next: the "outside factories"—the suppliers and distributors who are such an important part of the overall supply chain.

CHAPTER TEN

Supply Chain—The Muscle and Bone, Part II

"A company's suppliers, subcontractors, carriers, and often its distributors make up an indispensable portion of its total resources. This external infrastructure needs care and nurturing every bit as much as the company's internal resources."

To paraphrase John Donne, the English literary giant: "No manufacturing company is an island." Companies are like people; they don't exist alone, in a vacuum. They're dependent, enormously so, on other people in other organizations—*over which they do not have direct control.* These are customers and suppliers.

Over the years, I've talked with thousands of executives and managers of manufacturing companies. An interesting pattern has emerged regarding what they've said about their customers and suppliers:

- The customers are always unreasonable. "Our customers are really demanding. We have to jump through fifteen hoops a day to keep our customers halfway satisfied, so we can hang on to their business."

- The suppliers are always unresponsive. "Our suppliers ship us what they want when they want to. They don't care about what we need."

I asked myself, "How can this be? How can all of these companies have unreasonable customers and unresponsive suppliers? Many of them supply each other. There's a disconnect here."

The people were telling me *how it looked to them*. The reality is not always how it appears, and this example is no exception. The Golden Rule—do unto others as you would have them do unto you—cuts both ways. A given company is both a customer and a supplier. It should treat—and expect to be treated by—both groups in the same fashion.

For companies with more than one level of customer, e.g., retail customers and end consumers, the wholesalers and retailers are part of their supply chain. So are suppliers—and the suppliers to those suppliers.

A fundamental strategic decision for each company is how much of the supply chain should it own, i.e., how vertically integrated should it be. Let's address this vertical integration issue first, as these decisions are significant and define much of the operational environment. Then we'll get into the related supply-chain issues of make-or-buy, sourcing, and distribution.

VERTICAL INTEGRATION OVERVIEW

In a very real sense, vertical integration represents a macro make-or-buy decision. A firm wishing to grow a segment of their business has, broadly, two routes to follow:

1. It can grow "horizontally." This can be done by capturing market share from its competitors, by expanding the market via new products, and/or by acquiring a competitor.

2. It can grow "vertically" in two directions: upward—closer to the end consumer—and downward—closer to the source of the initial raw material.

In a mature business, horizontal growth can often be difficult to obtain. A good example is the petroleum industry, where the major players try to capture market share from one another. That's tough with a mature product, like gasoline, that's hard to differentiate from those of your competitors.

As a result, a few years ago some of the major oil companies decided to grow through vertical integration. They couldn't grow much further downward, because they were already drilling holes in the ground. So they integrated upward, taking over many of the retail service stations that had been leased to independent operators.

At the other end of the vertical integration spectrum is most of the electronics world. Many companies in the electronics industry are largely assemblers of purchased components, and their products are often sold through distributors and dealers.

In the middle: the automobile business. In general the product has a fairly high purchased component, but most manufacturers do their own distribution (via zone offices) to independent retail dealers.

Within a given industry, there often seems to be a norm for vertical integration; most of the players tend to do it to about the same degree. Certainly there are exceptions. IBM in electronics and General Motors in the car business are more vertically integrated downward than most of their competition. However, most companies in most industries will tend to follow a similar pattern.

It makes sense. The economics of doing business in a given industry are much the same for most companies. Second, other reasons to integrate will also impact somewhat equally upon most companies in an industry. In addition to growth, these reasons include control over quality, cost, and delivery.

VERTICAL INTEGRATION—DOWNWARD

In general, winning companies tend to be no more or less vertically integrated downward than the other companies in their industry. Instead, they create a competitive advantage through two strategies:

1. In most cases, the elements of the product that form its heart are produced in-house, enabling the company to differentiate its products from those of the competition. In some cases, of course, the product and/or the processes involved are proprietary. Often they're not proprietary, but are considered too strategically important to outsource.

2. Winning companies establish close "partnership" relationships with suppliers and carriers. Most—in some cases all— of the benefits of vertical integration can be realized without the disadvantages of actual ownership. These disadvantages can include the investment required, relative loss of flexibility, and diversion of management attention and focus away from the main-line business.

We'll return to the supplier partnership issue in a bit, but first let's talk about make-or-buy.

Make-or-Buy

The make-or-buy decision is a smaller, micro version of the vertical integration issue. An example of a vertical integration question is "Should we continue to operate our own foundry, or should we buy all the castings from outside?" A make-or-buy question is "Should we make this particular casting in our foundry, or should we buy it?"

As with vertical integration, much of the decision making relative to make-or-buy over the years has been financially focused. And I'm not so sure that's the best way to do it. An overreliance on financial analyses, excluding or downplaying other important factors, has contributed heavily to the "hollowing" of American industry.[1] Hollowing—making less and less, buying more and more—is an extremely high-risk strategy for a firm. The reason: Most things that you can buy can also be bought by your competitors, and they do not yield a competitive advantage over the long run. Buying almost everything, making hardly anything, prevents companies from developing unique skills and capabilities—bedrock attributes which Hewlett-Packard refers to as "core competencies."

Along with this financial overemphasis, cost-accounting systems in many cases have generated misleading information regarding product and component costs (this is gone into in detail in Chapter 11, "Measurements.") We've overemphasized the wrong thing—direct labor—and in the process have used faulty information. Is it any wonder so many bad make-or-buy decisions have been made over the years?

Winning companies tend to do it differently.

The bedrock question for any decision on make-or-buy, or vertical integration for that matter, is *"Does it support the strategy?"* As we've said, this is the ultimate "hurdle rate." If the answer is no, then why consider it? No matter how good the numbers look, it makes little sense to do something that runs counter to the fundamental strategic game plan of the business.

Example: a process which, done in-house, takes much less time than if sourced outside. A company could legitimately decide to bring that process inside, for reasons of flexibility and responsiveness to customer needs—even though doing it inside *may cost more*. This could be the case in a company where flexibility ranked significantly higher than cost in their trade-off analysis, which is described in Appendix C.

Supplier Partnerships

A major part of the quiet revolution taking place in manufacturing companies around the world concerns the relationship between companies and their suppliers.

TRADE-OFF ALERT: The conventional wisdom says that a company should be multiple-sourced whenever possible. Buy the same item from more than one supplier. If two suppliers are good, then three will probably be better. But doesn't this run counter to the idea of supplier partnerships, close working relationships, and suppliers as members of the design teams? Isn't there a trade-off between quality, cost, and delivery on the one hand, and supplier partnerships on the other?

It certainly seems that way. But nothing could be further from the truth. Let's see why.

The traditional reasons given for multiple-sourcing included:

1. Price. "If we can play one supplier off against another, then we can get a better price. We can use each supplier to keep the others honest."

2. Quality. "If Supplier A starts to ship us bad-quality material, we can shift all of the volume to Supplier B and/or Supplier C until Supplier A cleans up its act."

3. Delivery. "If Supplier B has a flood, or an earthquake, or a hurricane, or a strike, then we can temporarily get all of our requirements from Supplier A."

Make sense? It did then. Now, however, we see the winning companies doing it differently.

Over the last twenty years, I've been in contact with purchasing and manufacturing professionals from winning companies in North America, Europe, and Japan. Virtually all of these companies have a policy of single-sourcing wherever possible. Dramatic reductions in the size of the supplier base have been accomplished; these companies are buying from far fewer suppliers than before.

Why have they taken this step? There are three significant reasons for it, and you just might know what they are: price, quality, and delivery. That's right: The objectives are the same; it's the approach that's radically different. Here's how it goes:

1. *Price.* As a company consolidates its volume into fewer suppliers, it becomes more practical for the suppliers to get into constant, repetitive production. When they can do that, the learning curve effect kicks in; their costs and prices should come down.

However, there's more than just the learning curve at work here. More volume in a given supplier will often make it easier for them to create cells, thereby eliminating non-value-adding activities like moves and queues. In addition to costs going down, lead times should drop dramatically.

Last and certainly not least, consolidation of volume will often make it more practical for the supplier to invest in new equipment. This can drive down costs even further, streamline the supplier's processes, and reduce lead times.

2. *Quality*. All of the above factors—repetitive production, learning curve, cellular flow production, newer and better equipment—can yield enormous benefits in quality as well as price. High quality and low cost move in the same direction, remember? They're mutually supportive.

3. *Delivery*. What we've said so far is all well and good, but what about the potential for shutting down our plant when a single-source supplier has that flood or earthquake?

Right. There are three parts to the answer. The first is a disclaimer, as follows: I'm not aware of any company that is 100 percent single-sourced on 100 percent of its components and materials. Even within the winning companies, some items are felt to be so critical and/or so difficult for the suppliers to produce that multiple sources are considered mandatory.

Second, when close customer-supplier partnerships exist, the suppliers are very aware that they're the single source and that they must continue to ship per the schedule. In some cases, when a disaster occurred, the supplier's people have been able to "work miracles" to keep the flow of its product going to the customer—because they understood the nature of the relationship. In other cases, the single-source supplier can make backup arrangements with a sister plant on the other coast, or in another country.

Third, it's often possible for the customer, the buying company, to establish backup between two "non-related" suppliers. Figure 10-1 shows a typical multiple-sourcing arrangement.

MULTIPLE SOURCING

Volume Split

	Volume Split		
	Supplier A	Supplier B	Supplier C
Item #1	60%	30%	10%
Item #2	30%	60%	10%

FIGURE 10-1.

A single-source arrangement designed to ensure continuity of supply is shown in Figure 10-2.

| | SINGLE SOURCING WITH SECURITY Volume Split | | |
	Supplier A	Supplier B	Supplier C
Item #1	100%	*	0%
Item #2	*	100%	0%

* Qualified as back-up supplier

Figure 10-2.

In this arrangement, Supplier B has been contracted to provide Item 1 if Supplier A becomes unable to ship. And vice versa with Item 2. Supplier C is dropped from the vendor base, or perhaps supplies 100 percent of some other item.

In our discussion on Just-in-Time, we saw the principle of "one-less-at-a-time." This refers to eliminating waste—defined as non-value-adding activities—in small increments. For example, if we have four suppliers for a given item, is there waste in the system? Yes, we have to deal with four different sets of people, do four separate negotiations, etc. Well, don't go from four suppliers to one in one fell swoop. Rather, take just one away; go from four to three. Check how well it's working. If everything's okay, take another one away; go to two.

Before you cut down to one supplier for the item, you'll need to look at the backup issue. What happens if the single-source supplier has that fire or flood or earthquake we mentioned? Can you establish adequate backup? If so, take another supplier away. If not, then perhaps having two suppliers for this item is necessary waste. Even so, look at what you've accomplished: You've halved the waste involved in dealing with four suppliers. Your quality-assurance people and your manufacturing and engineering people can focus their efforts on the two—or ideally the one—remaining supplier(s).

In the chapter on new products, we identified an additional benefit from supplier partnerships: the involvement of supplier people in the early stages of new product design. If your key suppliers aren't involved, it's unlikely that your design processes will be as effective as those of your competitors who do involve them.

Supplier Scheduling

Most companies that build close working relationships with their suppliers make major changes in how they communicate with them. Why? Because traditional communication methods between customer and supplier are often inefficient, error-prone, and wasteful.

Think for a moment about what usually happens when a company orders component items or raw materials. The planner sends a purchase requisition to the buyer. The buyer generates a purchase order and sends it to the supplier's Sales Department, which in turn communicates with the planner in the supplier's plant. All of this has to happen before the supplier starts production. Further, if there's a problem at the supplier's plant, the cycle must be repeated, often more than once. These overly complex and cumbersome communications are unnecessary. They're also the method most frequently used in American industry today, simply because it grew up that way.

Today, most winning companies develop long-term contracts with their suppliers and then routinely communicate their schedules to them.

Some of these contracts are for a fixed period of time into the future, say one or two years, while others are open-ended. Some contracts are multi-page documents, with a fair amount of "legalese," while others consist of two elements: a letter from the supplier confirming the prices, and a handshake. Take your pick.

In the supplier scheduling environment, what happens to purchase requisitions and hard-copy purchase orders? Answer: They disappear. As with the purchase requisitions, they're no longer needed. And here again hundreds, perhaps thousands of pieces of paper per year can be eliminated. This is how companies move toward the desirable goal of "paperless purchasing."

Companies that have become proficient with Just-in-Time find that they're often able to use kanban in conjunction with the supplier schedule. Frequently this means that the schedule tells the supplier what to make, while kanban tells the supplier when to make it and when to ship it.

What's all the excitement about using Electronic Data Interchange (EDI) with suppliers? The good news is that EDI can help to speed communications and further strengthen the customer/ supplier linkage. The bad news is that some companies have mistaken the medium for the message. They have made the assumption, often implicit, that when bad information is transmitted electronically, somehow it will magically become valid. Only when a company can routinely generate and maintain valid schedules will EDI transmission be truly helpful. The old rule "Garbage in, garbage out" has not been repealed simply because one can transmit that garbage to a remote location at the speed of light.

It's important to get one's internal operations under control and learn how to schedule them properly first, because internal schedules generate purchase requirements. Only then should a company generate supplier schedules and/or begin to use kanban with the suppliers.

The people on both ends of the process—purchasing people and suppliers—need to learn how to do their jobs with these tools. When the purchase requirements are consistently valid, and when their expediting is one-tenth or less than what it used to be, that's a good time to get started with EDI.[2] The computer is always the "C item."

Let's wrap up our discussion of supplier relationships with a quick look at a company that's doing lots of things right, including purchasing.

Excellence in Action:

XEROX CORPORATION, WEBSTER, NEW YORK

Xerox is one of the world's most successful companies in developing supplier partnerships. They make effective use of the tools—Total Quality, Just-in-Time, Supplier Scheduling—and they work very hard at cultivating and maintaining long-term relationships with their suppliers.

It would be nice to say that Xerox initiated this change due to their superior insights and enlightenment. Well, maybe. But the main reason is that by the early 1980s, the Japanese were giving them fits. My associate Jerry Clement, a long-term Xerox guy until several years ago, puts it succinctly: "The Japanese weren't eating our lunch. They had finished with lunch. They were starting to eat our dinner."

Someone once said that fear focuses the mind, and the folks at Xerox really got focused. They transformed their company and have become once again the preeminent copier manufacturer in the world.

One of the interesting aspects of this transformation deals with a reduction in the number of suppliers. Xerox shrunk its worldwide supplier base from over five thousand in 1981 to several hundred by 1985. Why did they do that? Were they unhappy with all of those suppliers? No, not at all. The three reasons why they did it should sound familiar: price, quality, and delivery. And quality was first among equals.

A Xerox purchasing manager, citing his experience in the supplier quality process at Xerox, says, "There was no way we could work closely enough with five thousand suppliers, to teach them what they needed to learn about Total Quality so that they could deliver the high-quality, low-cost components we needed to be competitive. A few hundred suppliers, that's a different story. We could 'get our arms around them' and really form effective supplier partnerships."

Xerox spent enormous dollars on this supplier quality process. Their internal consultants spent many man-years in educating and training and helping those suppliers who "made the cut." So why'd they do it, altruism? No, survival. Xerox was fighting for its life.

Let's look at some of their results, keeping in mind that more than 80 percent of Xerox's costs of production is in purchased materials:

- Quality is up dramatically. Overall defect rates dropped from 10,000 parts per million in 1980 to 360 in 1989. During the same period, defects found in finished products dropped 78 percent, from 36 to 8—in machines that can contain up to 30,000 parts.

- Product costs were cut more than half.

- Xerox has recaptured substantial market share from the Japanese. David Kearns, the former CEO, wrote to his stockholders: "We may be the only American company in an industry targeted by the Japanese to actually regain market share without the aid of tariff protection or other government help."

Let's sum up our discussion of supplier partnerships with this point: **CUSTOMER-SUPPLIER TEAMWORK IS FAR SUPERIOR TO ARMS-LENGTH, ADVERSARIAL RELATIONSHIPS.**

VERTICAL INTEGRATION—UPWARD

Upward means just that—closer to the ultimate consumer. In the chapter on the marketplace, we talked quite a bit about customer linkages and connectivity, so let's confine ourselves here to looking at issues of actual ownership.

Upward vertical integration refers to acquiring more of the manufacturing and/or distribution resources between one's own company and the end consumer. As with downward vertical integration, we don't see any major differences here between the winning companies and the others.

There are, however, several trends worth pointing out. The first is that companies today appear more willing to make changes in their distributor/dealer arrangements when those parties aren't supporting the end customer as well as they should. They seem to be less willing to go along with substandard performance in the customer satisfaction area. Many informed observers believe that, by the year 2000, the composition of the entire supply chain will have changed. Many distributors will be out of business. Mass merchandisers and major retailers will become even more powerful than today.

Second, there's been a substantial reduction in the number of company-owned warehouses. Companies that used to have a master warehouse at their plant and three warehouses in the field may now be shipping all customer orders from the plant warehouse. Companies with eight field warehouses in 1980 may now have three. Companies with three layers of warehousing—plant warehouse, regional distribution centers, and satellite warehouses— may have eliminated the regional centers and now ship to the satellite warehouses directly from the plant.

Customer Partnerships

Think back to our discussion of customer connectivity—linking with customers, close working relationships, having visibility into their future requirements. Isn't that the mirror image of what we've just talked about regarding suppliers? Perhaps a version of the Golden Rule applies: Let's treat our suppliers as we would like our customers to treat us.

My colleague Pete Skurla puts it this way: "Ask yourself a few tough questions. First, is there someone in our supplier's company who has to forecast our requirements? If yes, is it a tough job? If yes, why do we make them do it? Why don't we help them to help us? Why don't we deal with them in the same way we'd like our customers to treat us?"

More and more, we're seeing customer/supplier teamwork extend beyond a two-level relationship. One example might be primary materials producers—e.g., chemicals or metals—working closely with their customers who are converters—e.g., pharmaceutical or fabricators/assemblers—who in turn are closely connected with their customers, the distributors, and they in turn are linked with their customers, the retail stores. These kinds of arrangements are sometimes called "Supply Chain Management."

In this four-tier arrangement, does ownership matter a great deal? Can't these arrangements work well regardless of whether they're all owned by one company or are all independent? Answer: Sure they can. The important thing is that people work together toward a common goal, with valid information and the right tools to do the job.

Ten years ago, most companies, found it very difficult to establish close working relationships with their customers. Very few companies were in "receive mode" to effect this kind of seemingly radical change. This was the era of arms-length dealings—often adversarial—and multiple quotes for each purchase order. But, as we've seen, the times they are a-changin'.

Here's an example, from the consumer package goods field. Over the years, manufacturers have "trained" their trade customers not to buy at the standard wholesale price, but to wait for the "deals" that are offered periodically throughout the year. *Business Week* said: "With all the wheeling and dealing, there is mounting evidence that promotions seriously distort the supermarket business. Supermarkets now need warehouses to store 'deal' merchandise, transportation to ship it, and office clerks to make sure [they're] getting the most out of each deal."[3]

This tactic amounts to taking products with very linear demand by the end consumer—paper towels, aspirin tablets, razor blades, etc.—and inducing massive demand surges at the wholesale level. Of course, this also leads to massive inefficiencies at the manufacturers' plants and warehouses. Both they and their trade customers are in a constant cycle of building up to meet a surge or winding down after one.

Procter & Gamble, an organization not known for flamboyance, is now at the leading edge in attempting to remedy this problem. They're offering substantially lower prices on products *permanently*. The aim is to break the industry's dependence on the deal cycle, with the enormous inefficiencies that result. This means "retraining" their trade customers to do the right thing: order only what's needed to satisfy the end consumer demand.

If this works, it will enable P&G and other manufacturers to become more efficient and cost effective. This in turn should lead to lower prices year round *for the consumer*—people like you and me who use paper towels, aspirin tablets, and razor blades.

Now let's look at a process companies use to replenish their own warehouses, and see if it might have even broader application.

Distribution Resource Planning (DRP)

Distribution Resource Planning is a set of planning tools, which initially focused on supplying inventory to field warehouses. Here also the mirror image analogy applies: DRP addresses outbound logistics while Supplier Scheduling is concerned with in-bound.

DRP is a time-phased logistics planning system, based on the same logic as MRP. It uses a statement of future demand (typically a sales forecast for each item at each warehouse), a distribution "bill of material" (which products are stocked at which warehouses), and inventory data (what's on hand at the warehouses, plus what's in transit to them). Utilizing standard shipping times and quantities, it helps people to plan replenishment shipments of product (or spare parts, or supplies) from the plant to the warehouses.

But it does more than that. Effective DRP systems also contain information on product weight and cubic feet. DRP can then be used to evaluate planned shipments in the aggregate, for truckload or carload lots, and also for space and manpower planning at the warehouses.

Andre Martin, one of the developers of DRP, points out that while the early DRP success involved manufacturing companies replenishing their own branch warehouses, its usage is much wider today. Many companies are using forms of DRP to plan the replenishment of inventories owned by their immediate customers: distributors, wholesalers, dealers, and so forth. And, as I implied earlier, wholesalers are using DRP for replenishing retailer inventories.[4]

In other words, DRP can be used *across* company boundaries as well as within. Similarly Supplier Scheduling, which started as a planning tool across company boundaries, i.e., to the suppliers, is now being used within the same corporation for interplant arrangements, where one division is sourcing components at a sister division. See Figure 10-3.

Actually, Supplier Scheduling and DRP are very similar techniques. They both do the same thing: They help a company substitute information for inventory and at the same time they help a company to deliver more dependably. They can *reduce, and in some cases eliminate, the need for forecasting*, with its attendant errors, because they give visibility into the customers' true requirements. An important point: **THERE IS MORE TO BE GAINED BY ELIMINATING THE NEED TO FORECAST THAN BY IMPROVING FORECAST ACCURACY.**

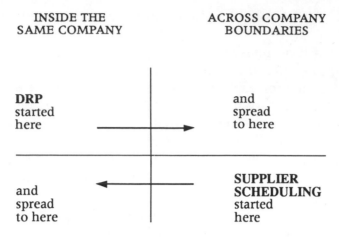

FIGURE 10-3.

Forecasting is wasteful, perhaps one of the most wasteful activities in a manufacturing company. It consumes time from key people, and it generates erroneous answers. These then generate additional waste as they affect subsequent decisions. Customer and supplier partnerships can help to reduce this non-value-adding activity.

Much of what we've said about dealing with suppliers also applies to carriers. After all, the carriers are suppliers—suppliers of both inbound and outbound freight. Winning companies view their key carriers in the same light as their key suppliers: important members of the total logistics team involved in moving the materials to the plant, converting the materials to product, and moving the products to the customers.

STRATEGIC CHECKUP

- Is it the company's practice to develop, nurture, and enhance core competencies? (Things that can be purchased outside tend not to generate a competitive advantage over the long run.)

- Is greater emphasis placed on close working relationships with suppliers than on traditional methods of multiple bids and arms-length, adversarial relationships?

- Are all decisions regarding vertical integration and make-or-buy first tested against the strategy?

- In addition to improving forecast accuracy, is effort being made to reduce the need to forecast by developing close customer linkages?

- Are you "training" your customers to do the wrong thing by routinely offering price cuts or other incentives at predictable times throughout the year?

Next: keeping score, and the importance of doing that correctly.

CHAPTER ELEVEN

Measurements— The Vital Signs

". . . the company's counterpart of pulse, heartbeat, blood count, and brain waves . . . Healthy people periodically track their vital signs; healthy companies do it continuously."

There's a largely bloodless revolution taking place behind what used to be called the Iron Curtain. Things are becoming dramatically different: What used to be encouraged and institutionalized is now seen not to work; what used to be forbidden is now accepted as necessary for the survival of the society. Freedom is replacing tyranny. Individual initiative is replacing centralized planning. Adam Smith is replacing Karl Marx. Today, it's "180 degrees out" from what it was just a few years ago.

ANOTHER "INDUSTRIAL REVOLUTION"

There's also a revolution taking place in manufacturing companies throughout the world. Things are becoming dramatically different: What used to be encouraged and institutionalized is now seen not to work; what used to be unacceptable is now viewed as necessary for the survival of the individual firm. The traditional viewpoint is no longer competitive. It puts companies out of business. See Figure 11-1 for examples.

This is a radical shift. It is also a fact; it's happening. The problem for many firms, however, is that they're still measuring performance via the traditional viewpoint. And since measurements motivate behavior, it becomes very difficult for people moving from traditional to competitive ways of thinking.

The measurement of operational performance is a strategic issue; it can dramatically enhance or inhibit a company's competitive position in the marketplace.

	Traditional Viewpoint	*Competitive Viewpoint*
Customers	Problems	Partners
People	Followers	Thinkers
Facilities	Okay	Showplaces
Suppliers	Adversaries	Partners
Quality	Acceptable	Zero Defects
Lead Times	Longer	Shorter
Improvements	Programs	Way of Life
New Products	Problems	Major Opportunities
Inventory	Asset	Liability
Schedule Compliance	Weak	Vital
Production Runs	Absorb Overhead, Minimize Setups	Just What the Customer Wants

FIGURE 11-1.

OPERATIONAL MEASUREMENTS

To be a winning company, it's essential to measure the right things and to measure them validly. Since the company's most important job is to create customer satisfaction, it follows that:

1. How a company measures itself can have significant impact on how well the company performs in the marketplace.

2. Many of the important performance measures will be operational, not financial, because the customers don't care about a company's quarterly results. And yet merely because a measure is nonfinancial doesn't mean it's a good one. One of the traditional measures of manufacturing performance has been "earned hours," i.e., how many standard hours worth of product has been produced. This is almost always counterproductive. It can result in people making things that aren't needed (because they result in earned hours), or alternatively, not making things that the customers have ordered (because they yield fewer earned hours). The customers just don't care about how many earned hours their orders contribute to their suppliers' scorekeeping systems. Nor do the customers care about plant throughput, efficiency factors, variances, or how much overhead we absorbed during the last period.

Measures of Customer Satisfaction

What customers do care about, in general terms, are the following:

1. Is the product free from defects? Does it work as advertised, or does it fail? Is it easy and pleasant to use?

2. Is the product available when they want it or, if special ordered, is it shipped when promised?

3. If special ordered, will the product be made and shipped quickly, or will it take a long time to get? Can they order exactly what they need, or do they have to buy a larger quantity? Will this supplier help them out if they get in trouble and need something very quickly?

4. Is the product priced right?

In other words: quality, delivery, flexibility and price.

Operational performance measures should center around quality, delivery, flexibility and, not selling price, but rather product cost. Note that three out of four of these are not financial measures, but operational ones. However, all three operational measures—when done well—*will drive down costs*. We touched on that earlier when we identified no inherent trade-off between high quality and low cost.

The critical issue is to view oneself through the customers' eyes. This means:

1. Learning specifically what's important to the customers so that these items can be tracked.

2. Keeping score by their rules, not yours. For example, many companies measure delivery performance based on calculations which make them look good, but which do not match the customers' expectations.

3. Using, where practical, external data—gathered directly from the customers—rather than data from one's own records.

Think of all the points of contact that a company has with its customers. Certainly these aren't confined to the sales force and the product itself. Other routine contact points can include the people in product design, the customer order department, the billing and accounts receivable function, field service, and planning and scheduling people in those cases where the customer and supplier are in a close working relationship. Winning companies measure their performance in these areas as well.

Xerox is one of the best in the world in measuring customer satisfaction; the company measures its performance as perceived by its customers via 55,000 questionnaires sent out monthly. But it also tracks *its competitors' performance as perceived by their customers* several times per year via the same process. This information is priceless, because it's coming "right from the horse's mouth." They learn how the marketplace feels about their performance and their competitors' performance, and thus can take action based directly on the voice of the customer.

Resulting Versus Enabling Measures

An effective measurement system must look at more than just these measurements, however, since they are results that are made possible by other factors. This brings us to the distinction between *resulting* measurements and *enabling* measurements. Attaining the targets specified by the enabling measures makes it possible to hit the resulting measurements. For example:

- "Six-sigma" quality[1]—how close a company is to attaining it—is a resulting measure, and is customer focused. The depth, breadth, and effectiveness of operator training on Statistical Process Control is an enabling measure.

- Zero back orders on the make-to-stock products—how close a company is to achieving it—is a resulting measure, and is customer focused. The accuracy of the finished goods inventory records is an enabling measure.

- Product lead times—from receipt of customer order to shipment—is a resulting measure, and is customer focused. The amount of setup reduction is an enabling measure.

Companies need to track both resulting and enabling operational measurements. Relative to traditional financial measures, they should carry a co-equal or greater importance; the emphasis by senior management should be on these. If it is, and if the execution is effective, the dollars will be there. The dollars will come, just as certainly as night follows day.

Effective execution involves communicating relevant information to the right people. The information on selected measurements—short cycle measures of quality, delivery, schedule compliance—should go *directly to the point where the work is being done* so that corrections and/or improvements can be made. **WHEN THE MEASUREMENTS ARE STRATEGICALLY VALID AND COMMUNICATED WIDELY, THEN THE STRATEGIC GAME PLAN IS TRULY DRIVING ACTION— DOWN TO THE INDIVIDUAL ASSOCIATES ON THE PLANT FLOOR AND IN THE OFFICES.**

Your company may already have effective operational measurements in place. Keep on using them, and refine them as you go along. If your company does not have viable measurements, there's good news: You don't have to reinvent the wheel. It already exists.

ABCD Checklist

The Oliver Wight ABCD Checklist for Operational Excellence[2] is a comprehensive measurement tool which contains both enabling and resulting measures. Today the fourth generation of the ABCD Checklist:

1. Addresses a broad spectrum of technologies and tools for operational excellence: Strategic Planning Design for Manufacturability, Just-in-Time, Total Quality Control, Manufacturing Resource Planning, and more.

2. Contains two levels of depth: overview (primarily for senior management reviews) and detail (for operating level analysis, problem resolution, and direction setting). Figure 11-2 shows an example of an overview question and its related detail questions.

ABCD CHECKLIST—Sample Series of Items

OVERVIEW ITEM:

14.0 SALES PLANNING
There is a formal sales-planning process in place with the sales force responsible and accountable for developing and executing the resulting sales plan. Differences between the sales plan and the forecast are reconciled.

DETAILED ITEMS:

14.1 The sales force understands the impact of sales planning on the company's ability to satisfy its customers.

14.2 Actual sales are measured against sales plans. Measurements are broken down into sales responsibility areas.

14.3 The sales-planning process is designed in such a way as to minimize the administrative impact for the sales force.

14.4 The incentives of the sales compensation system are effective and do not inject bias into the sales plan and forecast.

14.5 The sales force is actively pursuing customer linking. They are working with their customers' planning systems and communicating this information to the company.

14.6 Aggregate forecasts are reconciled with the sales plan.

14.7 Sales participates with Marketing, Forecasting, and Manufacturing in a demand planning meeting to prepare for each sales and operations planning meeting. A system is in use to communicate customer intelligence information to forecasting.

14.8 Sales areas are provided with useful feedback regarding their performance to plan at least monthly. Sales plans are stated so that they are meaningful to the sales force, yet translate into the sales and operations process.

14.9 The assumptions underlying the sales plan are documented. They are reviewed on a regular basis and changed as necessary.

FIGURE 11-2.

The entries in the ABCD Checklist tie in well to the criteria for the Malcolm Baldrige National Quality Award. One company with whom we've worked on strategic planning, Baxter MicroScan in Sacramento, is using the ABCD Checklist as the foundation for its Baldrige Award submission. (For more information on the ABCD Checklist, see Appendix B.)

A comprehensive set of customer-focused operational measurements is essential. But "the language of business is dollars," and we can't neglect it.

FINANCIAL MEASUREMENTS

In one very real sense, financial measures are even more important than operational ones: If you don't do them properly, you may get in trouble with the Internal Revenue Service, or the Securities and Exchange Commission, or your friendly state government, or all of the above.

Financial reporting requirements carry the force of law. They must be followed, and in doing so, companies must adhere to a set of procedures called Generally Accepted Accounting Principles

(GAAP). This is no problem, of course, because the Finance and Accounting Department knows how to do that.

There is one part of the accounting world, however, where the news is not so good. It's cost accounting. A few years ago, some of the North American manufacturing community woke up to the fact that their traditional costing methods had led them to make bad decisions. What's not as widely known is why. Lots of people know that "it's got something to do with direct labor and overhead allocation," but most aren't really sure of the specifics. Let's see if we can clarify it.

Problems with Product Costing

The following example is derived from a company that makes air compressors, and the numbers have been simplified to make them more understandable. This company has a plant that makes two groups of product: consumer air compressors and industrial compressors. The consumer product is relatively simple and has high unit volume; industrial air compressors are the reverse—complex and low volume, but historically highly profitable. The direct material and direct labor costs for these two products are shown in Figure 11-3.

	Material	Labor
Consumer Product	$ 12.00	$ 2.00
Industrial Product	$120.00	$20.00

FIGURE 11-3.

Overhead costs, often called "burden," include indirect costs for supervision, support personnel, utilities, and the like. In recent years, as direct labor costs have become smaller and smaller, overhead will in many cases be between two and eight times as large as direct labor.

These costs are normally charged to the products via direct labor, in this example at the rate of 300 percent. In other words, for every dollar of direct labor used to make the products, three dollars of overhead will be applied. See Figure 11-4.

	Material	Labor	Overhead	Total Cost
Consumer Product	$ 12.00	$ 2.00	$ 6.00	$ 20.00
Industrial Product	$120.00	$20.00	$60.00	$200.00

FIGURE 11-4.

Now let's look at unit volume: The company sells many more consumer compressors than industrial. As a result, much more overhead was applied to the consumer line. See Figure 11-5.

	Annual Unit Volume	Overhead Per Unit	Total Overhead Absorbed
Consumer Product	100,000	$ 6.00	$600,000
Industrial Product	1,000	$60.00	$ 60,000

FIGURE 11-5.

The consumer compressor was "paying for" ten times more overhead than its industrial counterpart. But was it consuming ten times more overhead? Probably not. Let's look at three specific functions within the plant organization: Engineering, Purchasing, and Material Handling. These are all indirect functions, and therefore their costs were applied to the products via the overhead allocation process we just went through.

Industrial compressors were much more complex than consumer. They involved many more engineering changes; well over half of the Engineering Department's time was spent working on industrial. But the consumer product was "paying for" ten times more Engineering support.

There were many more components in the average industrial product. About half of the purchase orders generated were for industrial, but the consumer compressors were paying for ten times more Purchasing Department time.

The consumer product line had such high volume that many of its material-handling processes were automated some time ago. As such, it used only about one-third of the Material Handling resource, but it paid for nearly 90 percent of it.

In summary, the company's overhead allocations didn't match where and how the costs were incurred. There was a disconnect between how the overhead was applied to products versus the products' consumption of resources.

Well, so what? After all, the company was capturing all the costs; the bottom line came out right. Did it really matter how accurately these costs were allocated? Yes, it did. It mattered a lot in that critically important part of the business called the marketplace. It seems the marketplace simply didn't want to buy consumer compressors at the price the company was asking.

The Marketing Department had set the consumer compressors' selling price at twenty-five dollars, because its manufacturing cost was twenty dollars (see Figure 11-4); they felt the resulting 20 percent gross profit margin was about as thin as they could live with. The problem was that their main competitor was selling comparable compressors for nineteen dollars—one dollar *below* this company's *factory cost*. This astounded the plant people, because they were convinced the competitor was not as good at manufacturing as they were. "After all," they were quick to point out, "the competitor doesn't even make industrial compressors, and that's the complicated product—really tough to manufacture."

Unless something changed, what might have happened? The company's sales of consumer products would drop until it was finally forced out of the business. During that period, the industrial product line would be forced to take on more of the overhead; its cost would rise; and, despite its "historical profitability," it too may have been heading for extinction.

Activity Based Costing (ABC)

What's the solution? In this example the solution was for the company to get a handle on their true costs versus what their thirty-year-old costing system told them. Activity Based Costing (ABC) was the tool of choice.

Activity Based Costing starts with the premise that direct labor is usually not the best basis by which to allocate overhead to products. As we just saw, products often consume indirect activities, and hence costs, in proportions different from their consumption of direct labor. Rather, ABC focuses on determining the *cost drivers*— the elements that cause the cost—for overhead and applies them accordingly. For example:

- The company concluded that the primary cause of costs in the Engineering Department was the number of engineering change orders written, covering both new products and changes to existing products. They determined that 75 percent of all engineering orders were for industrial. They decided to allocate Engineering Department costs to products based on the number of engineering change orders written, rather than via direct labor hours.

- They decided that there was a close relationship between Purchasing Department costs and the number of purchase orders generated. Industrial accounted for about 50 percent of this activity. They established the number of purchase order lines as the cost driver for the allocation of Purchasing costs.

- Industrial compressors consumed two-thirds of the material-handling expenses. Thus, the company selected the number of work orders kitted as the cost driver for material handling.

The company adopted Activity Based Costing and established the above cost drivers along with others. The result was that consumer products' share of the overhead dropped from $600,000 to $200,000, and industrial's share rose accordingly. See Figure 11-6 for the resulting shifts in product cost.

Things do look different now, don't they? The good news is that Marketing was now able to price consumer compressors at a point that could work in the marketplace. In fact, they had a choice. They could elect to match the competitor's price of nineteen dollars and

	Material	Labor	Overhead	Total Cost
Consumer Product	$ 12.00	$ 2.00	$ 2.00	$ 14.00
Industrial Product	120.00	20.00	460.00	600.00

FIGURE 11-6.

have a gross margin of over 25 percent. Or they could get aggressive. They could sell below eighteen dollars and still hold the current 20 percent gross profit margin.

Yes, there was bad news with the industrial line. Maybe, just maybe, it had not been as "historically profitable" as they had thought all along. With an average selling price of five hundred dollars, industrial compressors had gone from a high margin winner to a loser. Sure, that was bad news. But isn't it bad news that needs to be known?

TRADE-OFF ALERT: One could make a case that this company merely shifted its costs from one product to another. One could make a case that it needed to get out of either the industrial business or the consumer business. And one would be wrong. The issue became one of improvement to processes and products, to drive down the costs so that it could be a robust competitor in both markets.

Once the company knew where the problem was, then they could go to work on fixing it. Questions they asked themselves included the obvious one of raising industrial's selling price. But the more important questions became:

- Why do industrial compressors require so much support activity in Purchasing? What can be done so that we can become more efficient?

- Why do industrial compressors consume so much material-handling expense? What can be done about this?

- Can Engineering become more efficient in dealing with the current industrial product design?

- Does the industrial product need to be redesigned, perhaps using the principles of Design for Manufacturability, so that it consumes fewer indirect resources?

It's important to ask the right questions and, of course, to use valid numbers upon which to base decisions. Failure to do both has led a number of companies down very unprofitable and uncompetitive paths.

- Siemens Electric Motor Works in Germany[3] made standard motors and custom motors, the latter being more complex. A long-term price disadvantage in their standard line led them into a strategy of heavy automation to reduce costs—but that didn't work. After some years of low overall growth, Siemens decided it couldn't compete in the extremely price-sensitive standard motor business. But the culprit was not the low wage rates paid in Eastern Europe by their competitors, as management believed. It was Siemens's own costing system, which misapplied overhead costs and therefore erroneously reported that custom motors were highly profitable and standard motors were losers.
- A producer of writing implements in the Southern U.S. almost left the wooden pencil business—until, in conjunction with a factory focus project, they revamped their costing system. Now they can see that wooden pencils carry much lower costs than the old system reported. This has led them to lower prices on that product, one result of which has been to capture a substantial amount of K-Mart business from a competitor.

Let's return to the issue of efficiency. A significant benefit of Activity Based Costing is it *strongly supports continuous improvement.* ABC helps people focus on the source of overhead costs and which departments are the high-cost resources and which products are the big consumers[4] of those costs. Armed with this information, the people then go to work on reducing these overhead costs. Winning companies will apply Just-in-Time and Total Quality Control processes to indirect departments in much the same manner as they're used on the plant floor.

Other Uses for Cost Information

One of the reasons current cost systems are inadequate is they've been designed to support a number of different needs. One is product costing, as we've just seen. Another need is for information on cost control—the kinds of reports provided to supervisors and managers detailing actual costs versus budget that most of us are familiar with. Last, and most assuredly not least, are requirements for financial reporting to government agencies, stockholders, and perhaps others. This latter function includes the issue of inventory valuation, and hence product cost.

Here's the rub: Generally Accepted Accounting Principles do not require that there be a cause-and-effect relationship between how overhead is allocated and a product's consumption of the indirect resources. What's required is an accurate value for total inventory and a valid profit and loss statement. Many companies continue to allocate overhead via a direct labor base which has been reduced to only a few percentage points of total product costs.

It's okay to continue to do it that way—for financial and tax-reporting purposes. As we've seen, though, it's not okay for managing the business. This has led a number of companies to use more than one cost system: one for the government—with high accuracy in the aggregate—and one for internal decision making—with high relevance to individual products and processes.

This approach is fine. It will work well. But we're seeing this ABC technology develop so that companies can have a single cost collection and reporting system. The reporting side, however, will have the capability to display the information differently for the widely varying purposes of government reporting and product costing and control.[5]

What about that other need, for cost control? Well, not many companies set up a third costing system to handle cost control. One reason, perhaps, is that many current cost systems do a reasonable job in this area. A more significant reason, I believe, has to do with importance and emphasis. Robert Kaplan, an accounting professor at the Harvard Business School and a leader in Activity Based Costing, has this to say:

Cost information may, in fact, play only a minor role in operational control. A company maintains control best at the shop-floor level by frequent reports of measures like yield, defects, output, setup and throughput times. . . .[6]

In other words, information with units of measure other than dollars.

Here's the experience of an organization—in one of the world's most competitive businesses—that lived through the successful transition to Activity Based Costing.

Excellence in Action:

HEWLETT-PACKARD, ROSEVILLE NETWORKS DIVISION,
ROSEVILLE, CALIFORNIA

"Accountants tend to be pretty conservative and to view the company narrowly," begins an article[7] written not by manufacturing or marketing or design people—but by three accountants.

Hewlett-Packard has made a lot of progress in Activity Based Costing. One of the leading business units in this initiative is their Roseville Network Division, which makes components for HP central processors. Prior to ABC, Roseville had most of the classic problems regarding cost accounting:

- Manufacturing was required to collect data it didn't need, but which was necessary for the cost-accounting system.

- Manufacturing also monitored certain costs on its own because it wasn't getting the information it needed from Accounting.

- Most important, many people throughout the division didn't believe the numbers coming out of the costing system. When costing a new product, Manufacturing came up with different numbers from Accounting; Product Design's numbers were different from those of the other two.

Not a good situation, particularly in a business where new products come fast and frequently.

Much of the problem stemmed from how manufacturing overhead was allocated, since it represented about 30 percent of product cost. The system used at Roseville spread this overhead "like peanut butter" via direct labor hours, which was only 2 percent of product cost. Among other problems, this created an incentive for product development people to design direct labor out of the product—even when *the more labor-intensive process was superior.* Measurements reinforce behavior, right?

Marketing was unhappy, because many of their commodity-type products were simply too expensive.

Manufacturing, somewhat in "self-defense," created its own costing system on a PC. It was based on the principle that overhead costs be assigned to products based on what causes those overhead costs to be incurred. In other words, cost drivers.

Happily, Roseville's accounting people were open to change, and not hung up on "not invented here." They totally revamped their approach to product costing, basing the new system on the cost-driver approach used by Manufacturing. It was a fair amount of work, but they had "a little help from their friends" in other departments.

For example, they point out: "Determining what was driving costs for the various activities . . . may sound hard, but it was really just a matter of talking to the people on the factory floor. [Author's comment: also known as the "world's leading experts."] The drivers were usually obvious to them. Take axial insertion. What does an axial insertion machine do? It inserts. Therefore, the driver is the number of axial insertions."

One of the many benefits from this new approach is enhanced teamwork. "Engineers, designers, and accountants still argue—but over different things. We may dispute whether something should cost more or less, but how the costs come together is no longer an issue. We speak the same language, and the emotionalism is gone. Even the very precise lab engineers who may not accept the exactness of the cost-driver rates believe that the relative differences help them make sensible trade-offs between different types of components." According to one of their product designers: "Finally, we have numbers we can have some faith in."

A happy ending. But there's more: Remember how Manufacturing had to gather data they didn't need but the cost system did? And the fact that the cost system didn't tell Manufacturing what they needed to know, so they had to gather even more data so they could do their jobs?

Well, that's changed also. While always complying with corporate standards and with Generally Accepted Accounting Principles, they eliminated much of the data collection required of Manufacturing—including the reporting of direct labor. Direct labor no longer exists as a separate category; it's included in overhead.

As a result, they're saving *thirty minutes per person per day* by not requiring the reporting of direct labor time on individual products. Another non-value-adding activity goes away—and big savings result.

STRATEGIC CHECKUP

- Are at least half of the company's important performance measures operational, not financial?

- Within the operational measures, is primary emphasis on measurements of customer satisfaction?

- Are the results of the measurement processes communicated quickly to the people performing the activities?

- Are the company's product costs valid? Can they be relied upon for decision making?

Coming up next: how to develop and execute a customer-focused operational strategy.

CHAPTER TWELVE

Customer-Driven Strategy— The Brain

"Companies with a clear sense of their mission, with a vision for the future, and with solid strategic game plans will be far more competitive."

One of the shortcomings in the traditional approach to strategic planning is that it's often decoupled from the day-to-day process of running the business. The Greenbrier Syndrome, the practice of taking the executive team to a resort area for a week, every year or two, to "do strategy," often results in an elaborate series of documents, contained in a fancy binder. The binder goes on the shelf and gathers dust for the next twelve to twenty-four months. At that time, it's taken off the shelf, dusted off, and the cycle repeats itself.

I'm totally in favor of going away for a few days or a week to work on strategy. What I'm arguing against is doing strategic planning on those jaunts only, then letting it lie until the next session and not having it impact the way the business is run in the interim.

In the 1990s and beyond, that "retreat mind-set" won't work. Strategy is too important and too urgent to be treated as an infrequent event. Rather, strategic planning is a *process* that should become an integral part of managing the business, impacting how the business is run, on a continuing basis. *Strategy that does not drive action is a waste of time.*

Some people challenge the need to spend the time and effort on strategic planning. They challenge it on several counts, one being the lack of success resulting from the "strategy fad" of the 1970s. This was the period when strategic planning was controlled by large central staffs at the corporate office—with little or no real involvement by the line organization—as epitomized by companies like General Electric and Westinghouse. Of course it didn't work; they weren't doing it right.

Other critics of strategic planning point out that some companies have achieved a high level of excellence without an explicit strategy. And they're correct. Some companies have done so, but not enough of them. And you may do it—achieve operational excellence, operate with zero trade-offs, be world class, etc.—without an explicit strategy. However, doing it that way will be harder and riskier. Success will be much less certain to happen; the odds will be longer.

BENEFITS AND PITFALLS

By developing and executing a customer-driven strategy, you will:

1. *"Mistake-proof"* your *decision-making* processes.

2. *Increase your odds* for achieving success.

3. Achieve operational excellence *faster*.

4. Obtain *more benefits—in quality, flexibility, delivery, cost—along the way.*

With an explicit strategy, people throughout the organization can clearly understand where the business is heading and the plans to get there. This understanding will help to *mistake-proof* their decisions and to guide their day-to-day, week-to-week, month-to-month, and quarter-to-quarter activities.

A broad-based understanding will greatly *increase the odds* for achieving the business goals. Further, it's likely that these goals will be *achieved faster*—for the same reasons.

The final point concerns getting *more benefits along the way*. When executing a customer-driven strategy, improvement initiatives will be selected largely on their marketplace impact. Early on, the company should start to make substantial improvements in its ability to provide customer satisfaction—long before zero trade-offs are approached.

Another way to increase the odds for success and get more benefits quickly is to *be aware of the pitfalls*, which include:

- Complacency, the "We're okay" syndrome.

- Arrogance, the "not invented here" syndrome.

- Paralysis by analysis.

- Reading the ad copy instead of listening to the customers.

- Not working as a team, competing with each other instead of with the real competition.

- Overloading the people with more projects than they can successfully execute.

- Failing to listen to the world's leading experts: the people who are "hands on" with the product—designing, making, and selling it.

- Lack of focus and follow-through—putting the strategy on the shelf and letting it gather dust.

To those companies for whom these pitfalls sound familiar, I suggest they make them part of their past—but not future—behavior.

THE STRATEGIC PLANNING PROCESS

Over the years, we've developed a process to enable companies to develop and execute a customer-focused operational strategy. It consists of three primary elements:

1. The customer-driven strategy statement, spelling out the company's vision, its mission, and the primacy of the customer.

2. Measurements and tracking tools.

3. Frequent top-management review.

Let's look at each one.

The Customer-Driven Strategy Statement

If life were really easy, at this point I'd be able to provide you with a form where you could simply check the appropriate boxes and generate your strategy statement. Well, of course it doesn't work that way; life's not easy nor is running a manufacturing enterprise.

What I can do is to pass on the results of my experiences with companies that have made progress in this area. While the formats of their documents vary widely, there are some common elements:

1. *Define the mission. Why* are we here? What are we supposed to be doing? The word *customer* should appear prominently in this statement.

2. *Communicate the vision. Where* are we going? What will we as an organization look like when we get there? Here, too, the word *customer* deserves a prominent position. In this section, some companies have used the phrase "zero trade-offs" to define the long-term goal.

3. *Stress the importance of the company's people*, who are central in making all of this happen. Other core values and principles can be included.

4. *Identify the primary action plans*, the major initiatives under way or likely to be launched shortly, and explicitly identify *how* these short- to medium-term plans support the long-term goals.

5. *Keep it brief.* The strategy statement should be contained to one or two pieces of paper.

6. *Keep it simple.* Most people like to read things that are written in "sixth-grade English." Keep the jargon, acronyms, and fancy words to a minimum.

7. *Date it,* and change the date each time the document is revised. Companies that work this strategic planning process vigorously find that the strategy statement changes more frequently than they had anticipated. It should change. If the strategy is to reflect reality, it has to change over time because the operating environment will change: customers' needs, new products, new markets, competition, new technologies, regulations, improvement initiatives being completed and others being started, and on and on. The strategy will need adjustments, some minor and perhaps some major, to reflect the real-world changes that have occurred, and this may happen *more frequently than once per year.*

8. *Communicate it widely.* Spread the word. Some companies will present the customer-driven strategy statement to all of their employees in a series of meetings, give them a copy of it, and follow up later to see how it's settling in. (In some cases, the same thing is done for the suppliers, who are, or should be, members of the team.) The reason for this widespread communication is, of course, that it's difficult to keep the herd moving roughly west if they don't have a compass defining where west is.

However, the communication issue troubles some people. They're concerned that important information may now be available to their competitors, and that's certainly understandable. No company wants to disseminate truly sensitive information— regarding product plans, new technologies, marketing and promotional strategies, investment issues, and so forth. To the extent that this kind of information needs to be a part of the strategy statement, it can be contained on attachments and appendices that are confidential. Excluding this kind of information from the document under discussion here should not weaken its impact.

On the other hand, people are often surprised at the openness displayed by some of the leading-edge companies. Motorola certainly qualifies. It's one of the finest competitors in the world, in the fiercely competitive field of electronics, which has substantial Japanese participation. Explaining Motorola's strategies and methods, CEO George Fisher pointed out: "By the way, everything I just said, we have written out on cards which we hand out to all our customers and even to our competitors. This tells everybody who wants to know what we're all about and how we run the company. We're not worried about giving that to the competitors because *the difference is in the doing, not the saying.*"[1] (Emphasis mine.)

Yes! **STRATEGY WITHOUT ACTION IS A WASTE OF TIME.** It's the ability to translate strategy into effective action that makes the difference between the winners and the also-rans.

To give you a flavor for how a customer-driven strategy statement might look, Appendix D contains a sample, drawn from a company I've worked closely with on strategy development. It's very good—for them. But don't make the mistake of merely copying their material and substituting your company's name and products for the X's. Obviously, that won't work—for you.

Measurements and Tracking Tools

These tools need to address the following important issues:

1. How well are we doing in providing customer satisfaction?

2. How are we performing in other important aspects of the business, e.g., employee relations, asset management, cost containment/reduction, and other financial issues?

3. How are we doing in implementing the action plans that have been authorized? Are we on schedule and budget?

4. Are the specifics of our customer-driven strategy statement still valid, or does something need to change?

The first two issues are largely quantitative and are typically included in an effective performance-measurement process. The ABCD Checklist will support much of what needs to be covered and will point the way toward improvement. (See Appendix B.)

The third topic addresses progress on the action plans, the major initiatives under way. In this area, companies will often use a simple tracking approach, often one page per project, to summarize status, schedule compliance, performance to budget, and so forth.

The last issue—is the strategy still valid?—is more qualitative. The focus here normally centers around what changes, if any, are foreseen in:

- Customer needs and wants.

- Competitive behavior, from both current and potential competitors.

- Governmental actions, such as new regulatory requirements.

- Raw material pricing, availability, and other supplier issues.

Frequent Top-Management Review

Most executives work hard at keeping up with the direction of their business. Some do this very well. However, in many companies this process tends to be more informal than formal. There isn't a forum to bring the key players together, nor is there a focused agenda to support the process. What's been shown to work well is a periodic business meeting—the forum—with an agenda that is set largely by the measurements and tracking tools we've just viewed.

The details of this periodic meeting will vary from company to company. It should be done in a way that best fits the company's culture, the personalities of its key people, and the nature of existing strategic planning processes within the company.

Regardless of how this forum is structured, and what it's called, some basics must be covered. Certain fundamentals must exist to enable a level of strategy formulation, updating, and execution that will yield a competitive edge in the marketplace.

1. As with Sales and Operations Planning (see previous chapter for the details), this is a decision-making meeting. It has to be more than merely "show and tell." Within this forum decisions are made; these decisions lead to actions, which result in continuous improvement. It, along with the S&OP session, are two of the very most important meetings in the entire spectrum of managing a manufacturing business.

2. This meeting should involve all top-management people: general management, engineering/R&D, finance, human resources, manufacturing, marketing, and sales executives.

3. The meeting should be held frequently, at least every ninety days. It's no longer good enough to do the trip to the Greenbrier once every year or two and then not worry about strategy in the interim. Maybe that was okay in the past, but today the rate of change is simply much too rapid. About once per quarter is what it takes today to stay on top of things.

In 1987, when I started advocating quarterly strategy meetings, some people thought I was crazy. "Do strategy every ninety days—are you off your rocker?!" Today it's less controversial. *Strategic Direction* magazine, in the March 1989 issue, said it well: "Top management should take at least a day or two at the end of every quarter and discuss where they have been and where they are going. A little bit can go a long way."

Roger McMillan, Vice President of Operations and Finance at the Clarkson Company, had this to say:

We've learned to do strategic planning more often than once per year. Now we conduct meetings throughout the year, and it keeps the company's goals and plans fresh in our minds. All departments participate in the manufacturing strategy process, and they understand how other departments help each other in their work. We have progressed to the point where we don't have any independent departments anymore; they are dependent on each other. The more frequent strategic planning sessions have helped develop that understanding.

Under normal circumstances it isn't necessary to change the strategy every ninety days. What is necessary is to *look at the strategy* once per quarter and ask, "Is there any reason why we should change this? What's happened in the past three months?"

The strategy meeting can be structured in a variety of ways. It can be a stand-alone session, occurring about once per quarter. Alternatively, it can be integrated with the monthly Sales and Operations Planning meeting, with about one-third of the measurements reviewed at each session; in this case the meeting can perhaps be relabeled "SS&OP," for "Strategy, Sales, and Operations Planning." Or, once every one to three months, it can be appended to the weekly executive staff meeting. Take your pick.

What's important is that senior management be engaged, on an ongoing basis, in the formulation, review, and execution of the strategy. As stated earlier, it's not rocket science. It's running the business well, with a formal system for strategic planning and execution.

HOW TO GET STARTED

Developing a customer-driven strategic planning process fits the criteria we identified earlier for attractive projects: low cost, quick payback, high yield, and proven. For an average-size business unit of two hundred to two thousand people, about six months is typically required for the planning process to start to work well.

Early steps in getting started include identifying the champion, deciding on the use of a facilitator, and conducting the initial strategy meeting. Let's look at each one.

The Champion

Important initiatives need a champion—sometimes called a torchbearer—and developing a Customer-Driven Operational Strategy is no exception. The best person to champion this process is, of course, the general manager—the executive in charge of the business unit (president, CEO, managing director)—and yet sometimes it's just not practical for the general manager to head up the initiative. The process has been seen to work well when led by people who report in directly to the GM: executive vice president, senior vice president, or a vice president in charge of Marketing, Sales, Manufacturing, Product Development, Finance, or Business Planning.

The job of the champion in this process consists mainly of coordination, preparation, and motivation.

• Coordination involves the routine but essential steps of scheduling and chairing the meetings, ensuring that the agendas and meeting minutes get out on time, and interfacing with the outside facilitator if one is being utilized.

• Preparation includes developing the material necessary for the process to go forward: reviewing the strategy statement prior to each quarterly meeting for possible changes, ensuring that the measurement and tracking tools are valid and working properly, ensuring that reports on all Action Plans are ready for presentation, etc.

• Motivation means imparting urgency. It means making the process highly productive, so that the other people look forward to more participation. It means helping the others to view the business through the eyes of the general manager, avoiding parochialism, being sensitive to turf issues—all of those kinds of things.

The Facilitator

Point One: It's not essential to utilize an outsider for this process. I predict that some companies will be able to read this book and then proceed, on their own, to formulate and execute an effective, customer-focused operational strategy.

Point Two: Many companies find it's necessary to bring an outside facilitator in to work with them on this process. There are several important reasons for this: knowledge, objectivity, and priority.

The outsider must have broad knowledge of today's technologies and tools: the JIT's, TQC's, DFM's, MRP II's, and ABC's and so forth, and how they integrate. Often this knowledge doesn't exist within the company. (It's here in this book, but it's often tough to get people to read something they don't yet see as a high priority.) The outsider can serve as a teacher, imparting his or her knowledge to the group as a whole.

The outsider can serve as an objective facilitator for the early sessions of strategy formulation—where the group is involved in working the Trade-Off Matrix, developing the Customer-Driven Operational Strategy statement—and also later to help fine-tune the periodic business meeting process.

Lastly, the outsider helps the champion with the important issue of urgency, serving as a catalyst and motivator to keep the process on the front burner.

The Strategy Formulation Meeting

An important early step is for the top management team and other key people to get away for that three- or four-day off-site session which we mentioned earlier. This helps to "jump start" the process. I've been through these sessions both as a participant and as a facilitator; I believe it's by far the best way to get started, the obvious reasons being increased focus and fewer distractions.

Further, the facilitator should possess not only facilitation skills; he or she should also have a solid understanding of the strategic planning process and, as we saw earlier, broad knowledge of how the various technologies support customer satisfaction.

The primary objective of this session is to develop a working draft of the customer-driven strategy, including, of course, the vision and mission statements.

One of the tools sometimes used in these sessions is called the "Trade-Off Matrix." It's been used successfully by quite a number of companies, who've found that it helps to focus on how today's trade-offs impede them from providing high customer satisfaction. This information becomes important input to the formulation of the customer-focused strategy. The Trade-Off Matrix is described in Appendix C.

To sum up, the initial strategy planning session should have the following characteristics:

Participants: top management and other key people as appropriate

Location: off-site

Duration: several days

Process: a decision-making meeting, often with outside facilitation

Output: a working draft of the customer-driven strategy, including the vision and mission statements

Action Plans

Following the initial strategy meeting, action plans need to be addressed. Some major improvement initiatives may already be under way, and they should be reviewed. In most cases, these initiatives will be validated by the new customer-driven strategy and thus should be integrated into it. This should be done by explicitly referencing them in the working draft of the strategy statement. It's important that this be done; if it's not, people may start to wonder about the "XYZ project." They may start to ask themselves, "Is the XYZ project on hold, has it been canceled, does it not fit the new strategy?" and so forth.

New improvement initiatives will probably be launched as a result of developing the customer-driven strategy. As these decisions are made, action plans should be folded into the strategy statement so that, again, the people understand the what's and why's of the new initiatives.

In a perfect world, a company could pursue many, many action plans simultaneously without overloading its people. But the world's not perfect, and we can't do everything at once. Therefore, a company needs to be selective about which opportunities it pursues. The Opportunity Evaluator is a simple technique we've developed to help companies get a preliminary focus on these issues. Using some of the mechanics of QFD, it compares the relative attractiveness of various improvement opportunities from a strategic standpoint. The Opportunity Evaluator is described in detail in Appendix E.

The Workload Problem

In at least three out of four companies I visit, the people have too much on their plate. Too many projects, too many new initiatives, too many "balls in the air" with too little time to juggle them all.

In these cases, the company's purpose is to make rapid improvement. That's good. But the method is flawed, because when too many balls are in the air, some get dropped and fall through the cracks. With the best intentions in the world, the company has set itself up for:

- A series of unsuccessful projects.

- Lack of progress.

- Frustrated and burned-out people.

- Being accused of "flavor-of-the-month management," where the next TLA (three-letter acronym) is widely publicized before the prior ones have been successfully implemented.

The strategic planning process we've presented will help to eliminate the workload problem. One of the tools sometimes used here is called the "Workload Estimator," and it's detailed in Appendix F. It's rough-cut, not precise, but it can help get you "in the ballpark" regarding what's being asked of the people and what they have time to do.

Figure 12-1 recaps the three-part process for developing and executing a customer-focused strategy, and Figure 12-2 outlines some supporting tools to help in the process.

Developing and Executing a Customer-Focused Operational Strategy

---

1. *Develop the customer-driven strategy statement*—to communicate widely the company's vision, mission, and the initiatives it will pursue to achieve them.

2. *Establish customer-focused measurements and tracking tools*—to form the foundation for the next step.

3. *Conduct frequent top-management review*—to ensure that the strategy remains valid, that it's driving action, and that progress in executing the strategy is being made rapidly.

FIGURE 12-1.

Supporting Tools to Help in Strategy Formulation and Execution

---

1. *The Trade-Off Matrix*
   Purpose: helps people to focus on impediments to customer satisfaction.

   Function: input to development of the strategy statement and selection of action plans.

   Details: in Appendix C.

2. *The ABCD Checklist*
   Purpose: can serve as a major portion of the company's measurement and tracking tools.

   Function: used in both the top-management review sessions and also at the operating level of the business.

   Details: in Appendix B.

3. *The Opportunity Evaluator*
   Purpose: to help people select major improvement initiatives that support the strategy.

   Function: input to the selection of action plans.

   Details: in Appendix E.

4. *The Workload Estimator*
   Purpose: to help avoid overloading the people who have to implement the action plans.

   Function: input to the selection of the action plans

   Details: in Appendix F.

FIGURE 12-2.

Early in this book, we discussed the necessity of doing effective strategic planning at the operational level of the business. It may be helpful to restate it:

- To be a winner in the 1990s and beyond, a company will need to provide customer satisfaction that is superior to what its competitors are providing.

- To provide superior customer satisfaction, the company had better have a strategic game plan for accomplishing that. Leaving it to chance is terribly risky.

- This strategic plan should:

  - Be explicit.

  - Be focused primarily on the customer.

  - Drive specific actions for major improvements throughout the company.

  - Involve General Management, Finance, Human Resources, Manufacturing, Marketing, Product Development, and Sales.

  - Be reviewed and updated frequently.

The process we've presented here has these characteristics, as follows:

- It's a *formal system*, not informal. Done properly, it's planned and pro-active; it's a key part of "the way we run the business."

- It's *closed-loop*, not one-way. It contains feedback loops, to ensure that (1) the strategic game plan remains valid and (2) the customer-driven strategy is being executed.

- It provides *linkage*, upward to the business strategy and downward to the day-to-day operation of the business.

And, as we've seen, it promotes teamwork, an issue we need to revisit one last time.

WINNING REQUIRES TEAMWORK

We need help with teamwork. It comes less naturally to us than to some others—the Japanese, for example.

Can we do it? Certainly. We play a good game of football, one of the most interdependent sports ever invented. Good football teams have good game plans. If you'd like a non-sports example, think about what happens on the deck of a U.S. Navy aircraft carrier during flight operations—at night—in a heavy sea. This is teamwork raised to the nth degree.

Back to running a manufacturing enterprise and its need for teamwork. This is where a number of the tools we've discussed come into play—they enable us to operate with greater teamwork. Effective, ongoing, customer-driven strategic planning is one of these.

The strategy, containing the vision and mission statements, provides an explicit game plan. It promotes cross-functional cooperation; it helps people to understand the other departments' problems and opportunities; and it drives continuous improvement from the viewpoint of the customers—both internal and external.

From Mike Andaloro, Vice President of Logistics and Operations at Pioneer Flour Mills in San Antonio, Texas: "We have used [the strategy process] to help tie Marketing and Manufacturing together. We have a mutual understanding of how one impacts the other. Our company is much more action- and accountability-oriented and we are identifying problems that we didn't know existed before. We get to root causes of problems quickly and implement corrective courses of action—quickly."

Implementing a customer-driven strategic planning *process* in a company is important, and urgent. The strategy will help to "mistake-proof" the decision-making process. The strategy will lead the company into the intelligent selection of which technologies to pursue in what sequence, so that customer satisfaction can be increased rapidly without overloading the people.

All manufacturing companies need to use each of these people-based technologies and use them very well. To do otherwise is to place oneself at a competitive disadvantage against the rival who uses all of them well. All other things being equal, the company that makes effective use of these proven technologies will outperform the competition.

Your company can be a consistent winner in the years to come. However, to ensure this, you need an explicit customer-driven strategy. Because of competitive threats, domestic and otherwise, this needs to be done quickly. Strategy can no longer be viewed as an interesting intellectual exercise, to be done on those rare occasions when things aren't too hectic. Strategy is urgent.

Develop your customer-focused operational strategy, execute it well, and you'll win. You'll be better than the competition. You'll leave 'em in the dust.

Just do it! Good luck and Godspeed.

Marketplace and Financial Aspects of Reducing Setups and Changeovers

For most companies, setup reduction is the ultimate in a low-cost, quick-payback, high-yield, and proven initiative that can improve things quickly. Therefore, it's worth additional attention.

Please note: The following is not an example of a strategy. Rather, it's an action that would flow from the strategy. The purpose is not to make the reader an expert in setup reduction, but simply to present one example of what's possible.

Nonmanufacturing departments—such as Marketing, Sales, Finance, and others—can benefit greatly from what happens on the plant floor as a result of reducing changeovers. Readers from those departments may want to stay tuned.

Most manufacturing companies can reduce setup and changeover times by *75 percent or more,* without having to spend *hardly any money.* You can leave your Capital Appropriation form in the drawer. Figure on a few hundred dollars for a couple of reels of videotape (to film the current process) and for some copies of Shigeo Shingo's book,[1] which is the definitive work on reducing setups and changeovers.

Let's take the case of a consumer package goods company producing a product (perhaps cough syrup, or crackers, or candy) in two sizes: regular and large. One filling/packaging line, running two shifts, is used exclusively for this product. The changeover time to go from one size to another is twenty-four hours.

The company's scheduling approach is to run for two weeks on one size, then do a weekend changeover to the other size for a two-week run. Therefore, the order quantity for each product is four weeks' worth of sales. Also, the company likes to carry a one-week safety stock to protect against abnormal demand.

The average inventory for each product is approximately the safety stock plus one-half the order quantity. In this case:

Avg inventory = 1 week safety stock + half the 4 weeks' order qty = 3 weeks' supply.

The product cost averages $1 per unit, and let's assume that we sell about 250,000 of each size per week. Inventory investment, therefore, will be about $1.5 million for this product family (500,000 units per week, times 3 weeks, times $1 per unit).

Customer service in this environment is good. However, there are some cases where abnormal demand for the size not being run results in either back orders (making Sales and Marketing unhappy) or a midweek changeover (which makes Manufacturing unhappy). It's usually win-lose or lose-win. It's never win-win. It's sometimes lose-lose.

Let's say the company decides to "do something radical." Rather than continuing to do business as usual, they attack changeover times on this line. This is radical because most of us manufacturing folks have been taught to worry about feeds and speeds and high output. What the Japanese have done is raise quick changeover to equal importance.

Because of this, the first "changeover" has to be in the minds of the chief manufacturing officer and his or her people—to understand the importance of quick setup and then to establish this as a high-priority objective. Once this is done, significant improvements can follow. Let's take a look.

The company cuts the setup time in half, to twelve hours. Because they halved the setup time, they can double the frequency of setup with no additional expenditure of time. Now they can change over *each week* for no more money. And look what happens to the inventory. The order quantity drops from four weeks' supply to two. Safety stock might also be cut in half. Average inventory equals 1.5 weeks' supply equals $750,000.

Again, cut the changeover time in half, to six hours. Setup reduction of 75 percent is not breakthrough performance; it is a typical early result in North American companies that get serious about this. It's also fun. And look at the benefits.

Midweek changeovers are now possible, on the third shift. The company can run some of each product each week. The order quantity is now a week, safety stock a day or so, average inventory about three-fourths of a week's supply. Dollars in inventory are now down to less than $400,000.

Here's what's been accomplished:

1. Over $1.1 million in cash has been freed up, due to the inventory drop.

2. Between $200,000 and $300,000 of annual expenses have been eliminated, based on typical inventory carrying-cost percentages of around 20 to 30 percent.

But wait a minute! Remember that trade-off between inventory and customer delivery performance. Inventory reductions are fine, but usually they cause more back orders. Has that happened here? Have they impaired customer service?

On the contrary, *they've made it better.* Customer service has improved, not deteriorated. Abnormal demands won't bother them nearly as much as before. Now they're never more than a few days away from running a given product, not two weeks away as with the old arrangement.

And they shouldn't stop here. If they're smart, they won't rest until they can make some of each product each day. *Another trade-off bites the dust.*

Now, back to the money. What should the company do with the

more than $1 million of cash flow and the quarter million of reduced expenses? Here's what I suggest they consider:

1. Earmark some for the stockholders.

2. Send some to R&D/Product Engineering to help fund new product development.

3. Give some to the people in Marketing and Sales to help improve advertising, sales force coverage, market research, etc.

4. Last, *and certainly not least*, plow some of those dollars back into Manufacturing. Earmark them for the next improvement initiative.

This should become a process, not merely be a one-time event. A portion of the monies freed up by one improvement funds the next. And the next. And the next. Momentum builds. Excellence is free.

APPENDIX B

The Oliver Wight ABCD Checklist for Operational Excellence

The fourth edition of the ABCD Checklist is a listing of issues, opportunities, and measurements related to a company's operating functions, and thus its ability to execute its strategic mission.

For those of you familiar with earlier versions of the Checklist, a few words of explanation are in order. The ABCD Checklist has been around for quite a while, the first version having been written by Ollie Wight back in the 1970s. That first Checklist focused on a specific tool: Manufacturing Resource Planning. Back in those days, MRP II was the primary tool that manufacturing companies implemented to improve performance. Not many people back then cared about Total Quality Control; Just-in-Time hadn't yet crossed the Pacific; Design for Manufacturability hadn't been invented; and ABC referred to inventory control, not Activity Based Costing.

Over the years, the Checklist has grown in breadth and depth. The fourth generation of the Checklist, published in 1992, contains more than fifty overview items backed up by over three hundred detail items. It addresses all of the primary elements of a manufacturing business: customers, people, strategic planning, new product development, continuous improvement, facilities and equipment, suppliers, tactical planning and control, and resulting performance measurements.

The Checklist doesn't provide any direct answers. What it does provide are the questions that should be asked routinely—questions to verify that the business is being managed and re-sourced in a manner consistent with its strategic game plan.

The fourth-generation ABCD Checklist is available from Oliver Wight Publications, 5 Oliver Wight Drive, Essex Junction, Vt. 05452, 1-800-358-3862.

The Trade-Off Matrix

Before we get into the details of this matrix, we need to revisit briefly a couple of points from prior chapters.

First is the topic of competitive factors, subtitled "Why do customers buy our products?" We reviewed the following elements of competition:

- On-time deliveries

- Flexibility

- Conformance quality

- Product performance and features

- Product cost (via its impact on selling price)

We discussed trade-offs, first high quality versus low cost and how companies have made that trade-off go away. Next we talked about a trade-off that still bedevils many manufacturing firms: high on-time deliveries versus low inventory investment. Many companies use large inventories to enable on-time deliveries and also to help their performance on some of the other dimensions. Examples include using inventories to help provide flexibility, to compensate for unanticipated quality problems, and to allow for long production runs so that changeover costs can be held down.

But inventories consume large amounts of resources (capital, warehouse space, plant floor space) and can generate significant costs (insurance, taxes, interest, and utilities among others). When discussing trade-offs, we must keep inventories very visible. To do so, I'll include it with our list of competitive elements. Further, for purposes of simplicity, I've excluded product performance and features (performance quality) from this list. Now we have the following:

- On-time deliveries
- High flexibility
- High quality
- Low product cost
- Low inventories

Now we must recognize the timing issue. The long-term objective is zero trade-offs; in the short run, however, trade-offs do exist and must be addressed. As my daddy used to tell me: "Son, play the hand you're dealt."

Today's trade-offs must:

- First be recognized.
- Then prioritized.
- Then attacked.
- Then eliminated.

Recognizing them sounds easy. After all, trade-offs are all over the place. In many companies today, every one of the above competitive variables—quality, delivery performance, flexibility, cost, and inventory—is in direct conflict with all the others.

The hard part, though, can be getting people to recognize that the trade-offs are real, that they're today's facts of life. The people I'm talking about here do not work in Manufacturing (because manufacturing people know all about trade-offs). Rather, they have titles like president, vice president of marketing, controller, and so forth.

Here's where short term versus long term is crucial. My experience on this topic, which spans more than a quarter-century of hard knocks, is that introducing the element of timing into the discussion can make all the difference. When manufacturing people say, "We can't give you all of them—period," their words will not be met with smiles. Or attentiveness.

However, manufacturing people are quite likely to get their attention, and involvement, and cooperation, by saying, "We can't give you all of them today, but we want to do so in the future and, with your help, we can get there. Now let's talk about which of these elements are the most important to our customers." That's prioritization, and that's where this matrix comes in.

The purpose of the Trade-Off Matrix is to prioritize the competitive elements so that decisions dealing with trade-offs can be made consistently, and trade-offs can be attacked and eliminated in the most strategically effective sequence.

Let's look at a sample of the Trade-Off Matrix, as shown in Figure C-1. This one is focused primarily on the manufacturing part of the business.

Here's how it works: In each closed square, compare the two performance factors. Identify the one that is currently more important to your organization. If the factor to the left is more important, draw an arrow pointing to the left. If the factor to the top is more important, enter an arrow pointing in that direction.

The factor with the most arrows pointing toward it (either to the left or to the top) is the most important. These five factors can then be ranked in order of importance, and this ranking can serve two important purposes:

1. In the short term, on a day-to-day basis, this gives direction to Manufacturing when conflicts arise. In other words, when something's got to give, what gives?

2. Equally or more important, it provides focus on which trade-offs are causing the most pain and hence should be highest on the hit list for elimination.

THE TRADE-OFF MATRIX
Selected Competitive Factors

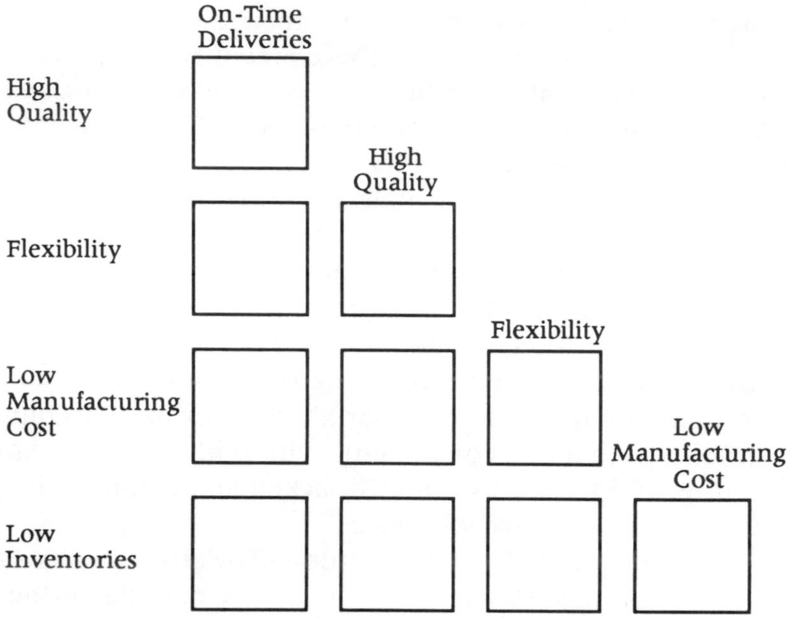

On-Time
Deliveries

High
Quality

High
Quality

Flexibility

Flexibility

Low
Manufacturing
Cost

Low
Manufacturing
Cost

Low
Inventories

EXPLANATION OF COMPETITIVE FACTORS

On-Time Deliveries—low/no back orders, shipping product
when promised.
High Quality—freedom from defects, not product features
and performance.
Flexibility—the ability to produce high mix, in short lead times,
with quick reaction.
Low Manufacturing Cost—only those costs that Manufacturing
can control.
Low Inventories—includes finished goods, work in process,
raw material.

FIGURE C-1.

Let's walk through an example. Visualize a meeting at the Mega
Corporation, Consumer Products Division (CPD). Participating are
the division president, Pete Prentiss, and vice presidents of Sales,
Marketing, Finance, Human Resources, R&D/Engineering, and
Manufacturing. Also present is John Doe, the group vice president
and Pete's boss.

The agenda for the meeting: Construct the Trade-Off Matrix for Product Family A, which represents about 60 percent of the division's sales. The group is addressing the top box, the delivery-versus-quality trade-off.

Pete Prentiss, the division president, states the issue succinctly: "Should we ship a product of less than desired quality to make the delivery on time, or should we go late on delivery to rework the product to 100 percent quality?"

Silence. After some clearing of throats and squirming in chairs, someone says, "Well, why would we ever allow ourselves to ship something that wasn't right? What kind of an outfit are we, anyhow, if we're going to be shipping substandard product?! What kinda lousy message does that send to our customers and our employees?"

It's hard to quarrel with that. Another person voices agreement. Then another, and another. During this discussion the manufacturing VP, Mike Moore, is taking it all in with a half grin on his face. He says, "Okay, you guys. I hear what you're saying. But do you really mean it? Remember three weeks ago, when we had a minor quality problem on that big order for Ajax Stores? What did we do?"

KAREN KIEFFER, the VP of Marketing: "We shipped it."

MIKE: "Right. And why did we decide to ship it instead of making it right? We all talked about it, remember?"

SAM STEFANO, the Sales VP: "Ajax is tough on delivery. They're a key national account, and we didn't want to make 'em mad."

MIKE: "Yeah, and what else?"

FRANCINE FISCHER, Finance VP, somewhat reluctantly: "Well . . . it was the last week of the quarter and we were under a lot of pressure from the corporate office. We'd already hit our dollar targets for the quarter, but then Corporate called and said that some of the other divisions were going to come up short and they really put a lot of heat on us to ship as much as we possibly could, so that's when I went to you, Mike, and gave you a song and dance and you were right in the middle of the whole Ajax thing with Kay and Sam . . . so we shipped it."

John Doe's face reddens; he opens his mouth to speak, closes it, shakes his head, and starts making notes. Then he asks, "Have we heard from Ajax yet?"

PETE, the president: "No, but that's not necessarily good news because the product is probably still in their distribution system. My hunch, though, is that we won't hear from them specifically on this, but that we'll probably have a higher than normal volume of customer returns. Ajax doesn't track customer returns very closely."

JOHN DOE, the group VP: "Does this kind of thing happen often?"

MIKE, from Manufacturing: "We average at least one fire drill per week. This example is only one type. There's a whole bunch of others, and they're all pretty well wrapped up in what's on this matrix. Maybe we should get back to that and see how we come out."

After further discussion, the group settles on quality as more important than delivery, even though they all agree it's a close call. (Left unanswered for the time being is the issue of how well they'll be able to live with this ranking day to day.) Pete draws an arrow to the left, pointing to quality. See Figure C-2.

The next discussion has to do with on-time delivery versus flexibility. Someone questions whether the two factors are really in conflict, and Pete explains: "If on-time delivery performance is more important, we should stop accepting customer orders inside of our normal lead times—which are pretty long, by the way. That way we'll have a better chance of shipping on time and avoiding back orders. On the other hand, maybe flexibility is more important to our customers. Maybe we should be aggressive here and

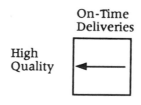

FIGURE C-2.

realize that we're going to have more late shipments. Karen, Joe, what do you think?"

After more discussion, consensus is reached for on-time deliveries. Pete draws an upward arrow in the delivery/flexibility box. See Figure C-3.

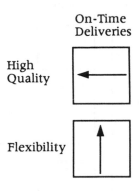

FIGURE C-3.

The CPD top management team—with occasional words of encouragement from John Doe, the group V.P.—completes the Trade-Off Matrix. The results are shown in Figure C-4.

Pete tallies the results. There are four arrows pointing to quality, one leftward arrow in the first column and three upward arrows in the second column. Quality wins. On-time delivery is next with three arrows, then low cost, then flexibility, and last is low inventories.

If the Consumer Products Division does it right, this priority ranking will become the marching orders for Manufacturing. It will provide significant benefit on two important dimensions:

1. On a day-to-day, week-to-week basis, manufacturing-related decisions will be based on this ranking. Quality will not be allowed to take a backseat to anything else. On-time deliveries will be given preference over everything but quality. And so forth.

2. The trade-offs have been prioritized for elimination. The most important trade-off for CPD to eliminate is that of quality versus delivery. The completed matrix indicates that eliminat-

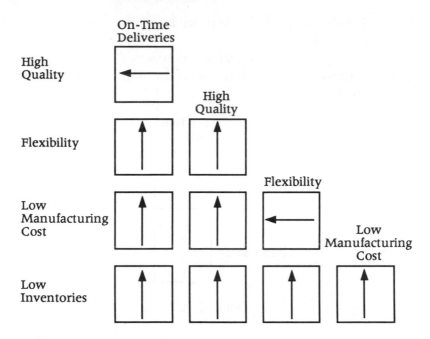

EXPLANATION OF COMPETITIVE FACTORS

On-Time Deliveries—low/no back orders, shipping product
    when promised.
High Quality—freedom from defects, not product features
    and performance.
Flexibility—the ability to produce high mix, in short lead times,
    with quick reaction.
Low Manufacturing Cost—only those costs that Manufacturing
    can control.
Low Inventories—includes finished goods, work in process,
    raw material.

FIGURE C-4.

ing this trade-off will make the greatest impact in the marketplace.

CPD should go to work on eliminating this trade-off, and its
operational strategy should explicitly state this. Other important
trade-offs for CPD include quality versus cost and delivery versus
cost; their elimination should also be spelled out in CPD's operational strategy.

It goes without saying that the Consumer Products Division of the Mega Corporation is not your company, and that's what's right for them may not be right for you. Your Trade-Off Matrix will probably look quite different from theirs. As a matter of fact, the matrix for CPD's other product line—Family B, 30 percent of the sales—may look quite different from Family A's. If so, it may call into question the issue of plant focus.

Take a few minutes and fill out the matrix for one of your major product lines. This would be on a trial basis, of course; really doing it requires a team of people, the way the folks at CPD just did it.

Sometimes it helps to work through the matrix in a two-step process:

Step 1: Develop the matrix based on exactly how you're doing things today (even though you may be convinced you're not doing them correctly). This defines today's implicit priorities.

Step 2: Review the matrix to reflect how you *should be doing things today*. If there are no changes from Step 1, fine— press on. If there are, make these new priorities explicit and start to run the business that way.

Now let's wrap up our discussion of the Trade-Off Matrix:

1. It provides day-to-day direction for decision making: When something has to give, what gives?

2. It prioritizes the trade-offs so they can be eliminated in the strategically most valid sequence.

If your particular company or division is in more than one market segment, then you may need to generate more than one Trade-Off Matrix. An example of this might be a company with an industrial line of products and a consumer line; the industrial customers, products, and markets could be very different from those in consumer.

Obviously, the matrix can be modified to fit specific circumstances. (It's even been used by an insurance company in the U.K.) Some companies may want to add product performance and features to the matrix, either as an additional competitive factor or as a replacement for one that's shown in what we've seen here, perhaps inventory.

The explicit priorities developed in the Trade-Off Matrix can serve as important inputs to both the Strategy Statement (Appendix D) and the Opportunity Evaluator (Appendix E).

APPENDIX D

A Sample Strategy Statement

The following is a sample of an operational strategy statement, developed by a company with whom we've worked. It has been disguised and modified for purposes of clarity.

XXXXXXXXXXXXXX - OPERATIONAL STRATEGY STATEMENT

Our Vision

We will continue to build the world's finest xxxxxxxxxxxxxxxxxxx-xxxxxxxx xxx xxxxxxxxxxxxxxxxxx, and will constantly increase our quality advantage over the competition.

Our Mission

Our mission is to provide the highest possible degree of satisfaction to both our distributors and our retail customers. This means increasing the value and dependability of our product in the eyes of our customers, and the value and profitability of xxxxxxxx representation in the eyes of our distributors.

Our Goals and Strategies

To accomplish this, we establish as our long-range goals:

- To design and deliver xxxxxxxxx, which consistently excite our customers and distributors.

- To produce products with zero defects.

- To always ship products on time.

- To produce products with the shortest lead time, so that we can excel at meeting changing customer requirements.

- To be the most cost-efficient producer in the industry.

Not all of these goals can be met today, but in the long run we must attain all of them. Therefore, we will adopt a process of Continuous Improvement. This will enable us to produce better products next month than today, better next quarter than next month, better next year than next quarter.

Our Continuous Improvement initiative will build on the progress made to date in our Quality Assurance Program (QAP), Manufacturing Resource Planning (MRP II), and Employee Involvement (EI). We will utilize new tools—Just-in-Time and Total Quality Control—to make ongoing improvements in quality, flexibility, productivity, and cost reduction a way of life throughout the company.

Our People: We recognize that the greatest asset and greatest competitive weapon of xxxxxxxxxxxxxx is the people who work here.

Through our Employee Involvement process—small work teams, education and training, skills development, and our Gainsharing pay plan—our people will utilize their talents to achieve all our goals. Our continuous education and training processes will include company orientation, product training, and the development of new skills.

We will make intelligent use of automation and new technologies. However, we will ensure that no employee is terminated due to productivity improvements. Layoffs may occur due to downturns in business, although we will minimize that to the best of our abilities.

Our Facilities: We will continue to maintain a manufacturing facility second to none in the industry. This attracts the best people, enables the development of manufacturing excellence, and makes that excellence highly visible to distributors, customers, and employees.

We recognize and are concerned about the external environment; we will continually look for and adopt processes and materials that are compatible with the environment. We are also acutely interested in our internal environment: Safety in the workplace is everyone's high-priority concern.

New Product Development: New products are the lifeblood of our business. xxxxxxxxxx must continually bring new products to the market—products that our customers recognize as having innovative design and exciting features.

Manufacturing and Purchasing personnel, along with our suppliers, play an important role in developing new products. They work closely with the people in Product Design from early development through the finished product. In that way, new designs become easier to manufacture, resulting in higher-quality, lower-cost, and faster new product introductions.

Sourcing: Suppliers are important members of our team and we will strive to establish close working relationships with each one. Suppliers are a key part of our overall Continuous Improvement process, and we look to them for ongoing improvements in quality, delivery, flexibility, and efficiency.

We further recognize that we owe our suppliers valid schedules, a win-win approach to solving mutual problems, and support in their Continuous Improvements efforts.

In our make-or-buy decisions, we will be guided largely by our objectives of stable employment. We also place emphasis on the concept of competitive advantage. We are prepared to produce in-house items that are difficult to manufacture so that we can produce them better than our competition or their suppliers. To facilitate this, we will establish a permanent Make-or-Buy team, composed of representatives from a variety of departments, including production associates.

Executing this strategy will enable us to remain the best in our business, and to constantly widen the gap between us and our competitors, making our jobs more secure—and our workdays more productive and rewarding.

Signed: _____   _____
_____   _____
_____   _____

Date:

The Opportunity Evaluator

The Opportunity Evaluator focuses on opportunities. A given company, at any point in time, can choose from a variety of opportunities for improvement. When an opportunity is selected for implementation, it's activated; it becomes an Action Plan.

So far so good. But here's the rub: A company can't pursue all improvement opportunities at the same time. It can't do them all at once, because there simply aren't enough people and enough hours in the day to accomplish them all.

Which to work on first? In general, the answer is those that will generate the biggest bang for the buck in the marketplace, in providing customer satisfaction. Other considerations include:

- How much will a given initiative cost?

- How long will it take to implement?

- How soon will it generate payback?

- How much work will it be?

The Opportunity Evaluator helps to focus on these issues so that competing opportunities can be effectively evaluated. In selecting Action Plans to improve the company's ability to provide customer satisfaction, the primary test is "Does this opportunity fit the strategy?'' If yes, then the opportunity needs to be prioritized relative to all the others under consideration.

The evaluator serves the following important functions:

1. It links project selection into the strategy, helping to select initiatives that best fit the overall strategic game plan. This is important, because a company can't do everything at once.

2. It provides a rough-cut measure of different projects, in terms of their relative attractiveness: cost and benefit, degree of self-funding, impact on people's time. Obviously, before a project is activated, a more rigorous evaluation should be made. The Opportunity Evaluator does not replace traditional cost/benefit justifications; it is merely a relative prioritizer. The format of the Opportunity Evaluator is shown in Figure E-1.

In Appendix C, we saw a fictitious company, the Mega Corporation, Consumer Products Division. They worked through the Trade-Off Matrix and came up with a ranking that highlights quality as the most important competitive issue; quality won four out of four trade-off evaluations. The complete ranking looked like this:

4 - QUALITY
3 - ON-TIME DELIVERIES
2 - LOW COST
1 - FLEXIBILITY
0 - LOW INVENTORIES

Now let's say the people at Mega's Consumer Products Division are considering implementing a Gainsharing compensation plan for the production associates. They're also looking at several other improvement initiatives and would like to get a handle on which ones are more attractive. To do so, they're going to use the Opportunity Evaluator.

First, they need to enter their trade-off rankings in the column so labeled. Please note the (+1) above that column; it means that we need to add one to the number of winning mentions (arrows). We do that to get rid of the zero, because we'll need to multiply all the numbers in this column.

OPPORTUNITY EVALUATOR

COMPETITIVE ISSUES	TRADE-OFF RANK (+1)				
On-time Deliveries	____				
Quality	____				
Flexibility	____				
Cost	____				
Inventory	____				
SUBTOTALS:					

IMPLEMENTA-TION ISSUES	RANGE				
Cost	<$100K >$1MM				
Payback Timing	<3 Mos >1 Year				
Payback Yield	<$1MM >$100K				
People's Time (x2)	=Minor =Major				
SUBTOTALS:					
GRAND TOTALS:					

FIGURE E-1.

The appropriate numbers, five through one, are entered next to the competitive issues on the matrix. See Figure E-2.

Next, we'll borrow some symbols from Quality Function Deployment (QFD)—we covered QFD in the chapter on new products—which help to identify relationships within a matrix. Positive relationships are considered good, and the QFD symbols frequently used to depict them are:

O —HIGH POSITIVE CORRELATION

◎ —MEDIUM POSITIVE CORRELATION

△ —LOW POSITIVE CORRELATION

Now the CPD people need to ask themselves: "What will be the impact of a Gainsharing plan, properly designed and effectively implemented, on quality?"

Let's say that, after some discussion, they conclude that it'll have a high positive impact on quality, a very positive benefit. That's a O . (You may or may not agree with these assessments. That's okay; they can vary from company to company. The important thing is to understand the process, so that you can do this for your own organization.)

Customer service, they conclude, will not be impacted as heavily as quality, but it will have a medium benefit from Gainsharing. That's a ◎ .

Flexibility: low benefit from Gainsharing. That's a △ .

Cost: high. O

Inventory: low. △

See Figure E-3.

We need to turn these symbols into numerical weights. A commonly used convention within QFD is 9 - 3 - 1: A high correlation is a 9, medium 3, low 1 (and no correlation is zero). This says that a medium relationship is three times more important than a low one, and a high correlation is three times more important than a medium. Let's stay with those weightings. See Figure E-4.

OPPORTUNITY EVALUATOR

COMPETITIVE ISSUES	TRADE-OFF RANK (+1)	GAINSHARING		
On-time Deliveries	4			
Quality	5			
Flexibility	2			
Cost	3			
Inventory	1			
SUBTOTALS:				

IMPLEMENTATION ISSUES	RANGE			
Cost	<$100K >$1MM			
Payback Timing	<3 Mos >1 Year			
Payback Yield	<$1MM >$100K			
People's Time (x2)	=Minor =Major			
SUBTOTALS:				
GRAND TOTALS:				

FIGURE E-2.

OPPORTUNITY EVALUATOR

COMPETITIVE ISSUES	TRADE-OFF RANK (+1)	GAINSHARING			
On-time Deliveries	4	○			
Quality	5	◎			
Flexibility	2	△			
Cost	3	◎			
Inventory	1	△			
SUBTOTALS:					

IMPLEMENTA-TION ISSUES	RANGE				
Cost	<$100K >$1MM				
Payback Timing	<3 Mos >1 Year				
Payback Yield	<$1MM >$100K				
People's Time (x2)	=Minor =Major				
SUBTOTALS:					
GRAND TOTALS:					

FIGURE E-3.

OPPORTUNITY EVALUATOR

COMPETITIVE ISSUES	TRADE-OFF RANK (+1)	GAINSHARING		
On-time Deliveries	4	○3		
Quality	5	◎9		
Flexibility	2	△1		
Cost	3	◎9		
Inventory	1	△1		
SUBTOTALS:				

IMPLEMENTATION ISSUES	RANGE			
Cost	<$100K >$1MM			
Payback Timing	<3 Mos >1 Year			
Payback Yield	<$1MM >$100K			
People's Time (x2)	=Minor =Major			
SUBTOTALS:				
GRAND TOTALS:				

FIGURE E-4.

Now we need to multiply the numerical weights by the value of the trade-off rank. For Quality we multiply the trade-off number of 5 times the correlation value of 9, resulting in a value of 45. So you're thinking: "Forty-five what?" Answer: Don't worry about that yet; 45 points.

Customer Service has a trade-off ranking of 4 and a ◯ for 3, yielding 12 points. Flexibility gets a 2 (2 × 1), Cost a 27 (3 × 9), and Inventory a 1 (1 × 1). Add 'em up and you get 87, as shown in Figure E-5. This number refers to the *relative* impact Gainsharing will have.

How much Gainsharing will help is one issue. The other is how difficult will it be to do it, and that's addressed in the lower half of the Opportunity Evaluator.

For a company of average size, like the Consumer Products Division, project costs are often considered minor if they're less than $100,000. That's low cost, and that's good. A big project might be one that costs more than $1 million, which is not so good because it's a lot of money for a medium-sized company. The CPD people estimate that the costs to implement Gainsharing will be in the middle. (Please note: These costs are the costs of *implementing* Gainsharing, not the ongoing costs of funding it. The costs of funding the process should be considered above, when estimating the beneficial impact on reducing product cost, and roughly netted against gross benefits.) See Figure E-6, which has a ◎ symbol next to the Cost entry in the lower half of the form.

If a project pays back very quickly, perhaps breaks even in less than three months, that's considered very good (quick payback timing). If it takes longer than a year, that's not so good. CPD estimates it'll take more than three months, but less than a year, to break even with Gainsharing. That's a ◯ .

If the annual benefits are greater than $1 million, that's very good (high payback yield). Less than $100,000, not so good. Gainsharing at CPD: estimated at more than $1 million per year. That's a ◯ .

People's time is a major factor, very often *the* constraining resource. There we give it twice as much weight; note the (× 2) next to it. CPD estimates it'll take a major amount of people's time to implement Gainsharing: Production associates, manufacturing

OPPORTUNITY EVALUATOR

COMPETITIVE ISSUES	TRADE-OFF RANK (+1)	GAINSHARING		
On-time Deliveries	4	◯ 3 = 12		
Quality	5	◎ 9 = 45		
Flexibility	2	△ 1 = 2		
Cost	3	◎ 9 = 27		
Inventory	1	△ 1 = 1		
SUBTOTALS:		87		

IMPLEMENTA-TION ISSUES	RANGE			
Cost	<$100K >$1MM			
Payback Timing	<3 Mos >1 Year			
Payback Yield	<$1MM >$100K			
People's Time (x2)	=Minor =Major			
SUBTOTALS:				
GRAND TOTALS:				

FIGURE E-5.

OPPORTUNITY EVALUATOR

COMPETITIVE ISSUES	TRADE-OFF RANK (+1)	GAINSHARING			
On-time Deliveries	4	○3=12			
Quality	5	◎9=45			
Flexibility	2	△1=2			
Cost	3	◎9=27			
Inventory	1	△1=1			
SUBTOTALS:		87			

IMPLEMENTATION ISSUES	RANGE				
Cost	<$100K >$1MM	○			
Payback Timing	<3 Mos >1 Year	○			
Payback Yield	<$1MM >$100K	◎			
People's Time (x2)	=Minor =Major	△			
SUBTOTALS:					
GRAND TOTALS:					

FIGURE E-6.

supervisors and managers, manufacturing engineering, human re-sources, accounting, and perhaps other people will be involved to one degree or another. That's a △ , because when a project takes a lot of time, that's not so good.

A brief digression: This is perhaps the toughest element of all to estimate. How much time is "a lot"? Will it be all extra time, or will some of the time required quickly replace what the individuals are doing now? For a given group or department, how much capacity do they have to handle multiple projects?

It's not easy, and whatever you do won't be terribly accurate. However, it'll get you in the ballpark, so that you can make in-formed decisions about how much extra work is okay and how much is too much. And that's a lot better than the overloaded master schedule that we referred to earlier. Keep in mind that this is all relative. In Appendix F, we'll take a look at the Workload Evaluator, and that should help a bit.

Figure E-7 shows the numerical weights assigned for the imple-mentation issues we just covered. Note that People's Time gets a value of 2, not 1, because of its double weighting. The subtotal for the Implementation Issues is 17, and when added to the 87 from the top half of the page, gives an overall value of 104. As we said, this score can be used to compare Gainsharing against other oppor-tunities evaluated using the same technique.

If this company is considering four other opportunities, and they all have relative scores in the 80s and 90s, Gainsharing will look very attractive. This does not mean they should decide to do it on that basis alone. It does mean that Gainsharing, in this example, should be evaluated very closely due to its potential as indicated by the Opportunity Evaluator.

OPPORTUNITY EVALUATOR

COMPETITIVE ISSUES	TRADE-OFF RANK (+1)	GAINSHARING		
On-time Deliveries	4	○3 = 12		
Quality	5	◎9 = 45		
Flexibility	2	△1 = 2		
Cost	3	◎9 = 27		
Inventory	1	△1 = 1		
SUBTOTALS:		87		

IMPLEMENTATION ISSUES	RANGE			
Cost	<$100K >$1MM	○ 3		
Payback Timing	<3 Mos >1 Year	○ 3		
Payback Yield	<$1MM >$100K	◎ 9		
People's Time (x2)	=Minor =Major	△ 2		
SUBTOTALS:		17		
GRAND TOTALS:		104		

FIGURE E-7.

APPENDIX F

The Workload Estimator

The Workload Estimator is a sanity check, to make sure that the people in your company aren't being asked to do more than they can deliver. Trying to do too much—too many hot projects, too many balls in the air—often leads to no progress. This is what was referred to earlier as "an overloaded master schedule of management expectations."

A company needs a way to avoid this trap, and that's the job of the Workload Estimator. It relates Action Plans, both under way and under consideration, to workload by department.

The process involved here is one of "translation." It converts opportunities under consideration and action plans into workload by department. Let's see how it works.

Figure F-1 shows a blank sample of a Workload Estimator. The primary groups within the company are listed across the top of the page; Action Plans would be written in down the left.

Once again, we turn to Quality Function Deployment (QFD) for symbols. This time, however, we'll be using different symbols from those in the Opportunity Evaluator covered in Appendix E.

In the Workload Estimator, we'll be dealing largely with negative correlations, i.e., how much work needs to be done. The QFD convention for negative correlations is the symbol X. We'll use one X to mean a relatively small amount of work, which we define as less than 5 percent of each person's work week (two hours on a

WORKLOAD ESTIMATOR

OPPORTUNITIES	TOP MGMT	PROD DEV	FIN	HUM RES	MKTG/ SLS	MIS	MFG ENG	MFG MGT	DIR LBR	PR'N CTL	PURCH	QA/ QC
TOTALS												

<5%=1/4 day per person per week=minor (X)
5–20%=1/4-1 day per person per week=medium (XX)
>20%=1 day per person per week=major (XXX)

FIGURE F-1.

forty-hour week). Two **XX**'s equal a medium amount of work, between 5 percent and 20 percent (between two hours and one day per person per week). Three **XXX**'s mean a lot of work, more than one day per week for each person in the department.

Let's work through an example. We'll approximate the workload that would result from a decision to implement a Skill Based Pay system for the work force.

To get started, we need to ask ourselves: "What's the workload impact on top management—high, medium, low, or none?" Well, the answer is probably less than high and greater than none; they will have some involvement, but it won't be enormous. Okay, is it medium or low? Possibly closer to medium than low. Once the project is launched—if it is—they'll need to stay abreast of it, perhaps show the top management flag from time to time, and provide leadership to the departments that are heavily involved. (This latter point will be particularly true for the vice presidents of Manufacturing, Human Resources, and Finance.)

	TOP MGMT
SKILL BASED PAY FOR PRODUCTION ASSOCIATES	XX

Engineering/R&D will probably have no involvement. Finance, on the other hand, will be moderately active due to the changes to the pay plan and their impact on the payroll. Human Resources will be very busy on this project, Marketing and Sales not at all, and MIS will need to modify the payroll system.

	ENG/R&D	FIN	HUM RES	MKTG/SLS	MIS
SKILL BASED PAY FOR PRODUCTION ASSOCIATES		XX	XXX		X

My sense is that Manufacturing Engineering, Manufacturing Management/Supervision, and the Direct Labor people will be heavily involved, Production Control involved a bit, Purchasing not at all, and Quality Assurance/Quality Control may get involved in some of the training.

	MFG ENG	MGT	DIR LBR	PR'N CTL	PURCH	QA/QC
SKILL BASED PAY FOR PRODUCTION ASSOCIATES	XXX	XXX	XXX	X		XX

Is this precise? Obviously not. (Probably some of you are unhappy with me for not giving your departments another X or two. You're probably right, at least for your company's own situation.) The mission of the Workload Estimator is to get a rough-cut estimate of the workload, not accuracy to four decimal places.

See Figure F-2 for a sample of a completed matrix, in a company that's considering Skill Based Pay, Sales and Operations Planning, a major initiative on setup reduction, Electronic Data Interchange with its major customers, and focusing its two plants.

Figure F-2 indicates that there may be a major overload problem in Manufacturing Engineering, Manufacturing Management and Supervision, and Direct Labor. Let's see if we can sharpen it up a bit, via some quantification. Once again, we'll use the QFD weighting ratios of 9 (for major), 3 (for medium), and 1 (for minor).* See Figure F-3.

The numbers put it into perspective: It's ten pounds in a five-pound bag for the people in the manufacturing departments. It appears they'll be horribly overloaded if these plans go forward. As a result, it's unlikely that all, or even most, of the objectives and benefits will be met. Even worse, the people themselves will probably get frustrated and burn out.

Obviously, the solution to the problem is to defer one or several of the manufacturing-intensive projects, perhaps replacing them with improvement initiatives centered in other areas, such as Product Development, Finance, and/or Purchasing.

The Workload Estimator is an important tool, because it addresses the critical resource on a company's journey to operational excellence: It's people's time.

---

* As in our earlier use of 9-3-1, I want to point out that this is merely a convention which has proven to be useful. Don't hesitate to vary the ratio if this one doesn't make sense to you. The important issue is consistency and obtaining a valid relative measure.

WORKLOAD ESTIMATOR

OPPORTUNITIES	TOP MGMT	PROD DEV	FIN	HUM RES	MKTG/ SLS	MIS	MFG ENG	MFG MGT	DIR LBR	PR'N CTL	PURCH	QA/ QC
Skill based pay for prod'n associates	XX		XX	XXX		X	XXX	XXX	XXX	X		XX
Sales & Op'ns Planning	XXX	X	X		XX	X		X		XX	X	
Setup Reduction	X					X	XXX	XXX	XX	X	X	X
Customer EDI	X		X		XX	XXX						
Plant Focus	X	X	XX	XXX		XX	XXX	XXX	XXX	XXX	X	XXX
TOTALS												

<5%=1/4 day per person per week=minor (X)

5–20%=1/4-1 day per person per week=medium (XX)

>20%=1 day per person per week=major (XXX)

FIGURE F-2.

WORKLOAD ESTIMATOR

OPPORTUNITIES	TOP MGMT	PROD DEV	FIN	HUM RES	MKTG/ SLS	MIS	MFG ENG	MFG MGT	DIR LBR	PR'N CTL	PURCH	QA/ QC
Skill based pay for prod'n associates	3 XX		3 XX	9 XXX		1 X	9 XXX	9 XXX	9 XXX	1 X		3 XX
Sales & Op'ns Planning	9 XXX	1 X	1 X		3 XX	1 X		1 X		3 XX	1 X	
Setup Reduction	1 X					1 X	9 XXX	9 XXX	3 XX	1 X	1 X	1 X
Customer EDI	1 X		1 X		3 XX	9 XXX						
Plant Focus	1 X	1 X	1 XX	9 XXX		3 XX	9 XXX	9 XXX	9 XXX	9 XXX	1 X	9 XXX
TOTALS	15	2	6	18	6	15	27	28	21	14	3	13

<5%=1/4 day per person per week=minor (X)

5–20%=1/4-1 day per person per week=medium (XX)

>20%=1 day per person per week=major (XXX)

FIGURE F-3.

APPENDIX G

Glossary

ABC Acronym for Activity Based Costing.

ABC Inventory Classification A method of categorizing inventory based primarily on dollar impact.

Activity Based Costing (ABC) An approach to product costing that accumulates overhead costs based on activities performed and then uses the causes of those costs to allocate them to products. It recognizes the fact that, in most businesses, direct labor hours are not good bases upon which to allocate overhead.

AGVS Acronym for Automated Guided Vehicle System.

Andon Japanese word for warning light or visual signal.

AQL Acronym for Acceptable Quality Level.

AS/RS Acronym for Automated Storage/Retrieval System.

Automated Guided Vehicle System (AGVS) A system that automatically routes one or more material handling devices, such as carts or pallet trucks, and positions them at predetermined destinations.

Automated Storage/Retrieval System (AS/RS) A high-density rack storage system with vehicles automatically loading and unloading the racks.

Benchmarking A formal process used to establish goals for improvements in processes, functions, products, etc., by comparing oneself to other companies. Benchmark measures are often derived from other firms that display "best in class" performance, not necessarily competitors.

Business Plan A statement of future business activity, usually in financial terms. It typically includes projections of sales, costs and profits, and is accompanied by budgets.

CAD/CAM   The integration of Computer Aided Design and Computer Aided Manufacturing to achieve automation from design through manufacturing.

CAD   Acronym for Computer Aided Design.

CAE   Acronym for Computer Aided Engineering.

CAM   Acronym for Computer Aided Manufacturing.

Cause-and-Effect Diagram   A statement of a problem with a branching diagram leading from the statement to the known potential causes. Syn: fishbone chart, Ishikawa diagram.

Cellular Manufacturing   A form of manufacturing organization wherein dissimilar pieces of equipment are located together, so that items can be started and completed within that cell. See: Flow Shop, Job Shop.

CIM   Acronym for Computer Integrated Manufacturing.

CNC   Acronym for Computer Numerical Control.

Competitive Benchmarking   See: Benchmarking.

Computer Aided Design (CAD)   The use of computers in interactive engineering drawing and storage of designs. Programs complete the layout, geometric transformations, projections, rotations, magnifications, and interval (cross-section) views of a part and its relationship with other parts.

Computer Aided Engineering (CAE)   The process of generating and testing engineering specifications on a computer work station.

Computer Aided Manufacturing (CAM)   Use of computers to program, direct, and control production equipment in the fabrication of manufactured items.

Computer Integrated Manufacturing (CIM)   In the narrow sense, this refers to tying together the "islands of automation" on the plant floor, via electronic linkages. The broader meaning of the term covers the integration of all information (engineering, business, and process control) involved in the total spectrum of manufacturing activity.

Computer Numerical Control (CNC)   A technique in which a machine tool control uses a minicomputer to store numerical instructions.

Concurrent Engineering   See: Design for Manufacturability.

Demand Management   The function of recognizing and managing all of the demands for products and other items. It encompasses the activities of forecasting, order entry, order promising, and planning for branch warehouse requirements, interplant requirements, and service parts demand.

Deming Circle   See: Plan-Do-Check-Action.

Design for Assembly   See: Design for Manufacturability.

Design for Manufacturability (DFM)   A team-intensive, people-based technology which is sensitive to production issues. It involves people from a wide variety of functions, and enables early procurement and production to happen concurrently with the design process.

DFM   Acronym for Design for Manufacturability.

Distribution Resource Planning (DRP)   A people-based technology aimed at effective replenishment of inventory at distribution centers, coupled with techniques for planning key resources such as transportation, warehouse space, manpower, etc.

DRP   Acronym for Distribution Resource Planning.

EDI   Acronym for Electronic Data Interchange.

EI   Acronym for Employee Involvement.

Electronic Data Interchange (EDI)   The computer-to-computer exchange of information between separate organizations, including schedules, specifications, test results, etc.

Employee Involvement (EI)   The concept of using the experience, creative energy, and intelligence of all employees by treating them with respect, keeping them informed, and including them and their ideas in decision-making processes.

Factory-Within-a-Factory   See: Plant-Within-a-Plant.

Financial Integration   Refers to the generation of financial planning and control numbers from the operational (MRP II) data base.

Flexible Manufacturing System (FMS)   A highly automated production resource, interconnected by a central control system, allowing for the production of a multiplicity of items and quick changeover.

Flow Shop   A form of manufacturing organization wherein dissimilar pieces of equipment are located adjacent to one another, based on what they do to the product. Examples include assembly lines, filling and packaging lines, manufacturing cells. See: Job Shop.

Fishbone Chart   A type of cause-and-effect diagram.

Focused Factory   A plant set up to deal with a limited range of markets, customers, products, technologies, etc. See: Plant-Within-a-Plant.

Gainsharing   A method of incentive compensation where employees share collectively in savings from productivity improvements.

Group Technology   An approach which identifies the "sameness" of parts, equipment or processes. It provides for rapid retrieval of existing designs and anticipates a cellular type production equipment layout.

Ishikawa Diagram   A type of cause-and-effect diagram.

Jidoka   The Japanese term for the practice of stopping the production line when a defect occurs.

JIT   Acronym for Just-in-Time.

Job Shop   A functional form of manufacturing organization whose work centers are organized by similar types of equipment, such as drilling, forging, spinning, mixing, compressing, blending, etc. Production jobs move through the facility based on routings that are specific to the items being produced. See: Flow Shop.

Just-in-Time (JIT)   A people-based technology focusing on the continuous elimination of waste. It encompasses all activities required to produce a product, from design through delivery and including all stages of conversion from raw material onward.

Kaizen   The Japanese term for continuous improvement.

Kanban   A method for Just-in-Time operations in which consuming operations pull from feeding operations. Feeding operations are authorized to produce only after receiving a kanban card (or other trigger) from the consuming operation. Kanban in Japanese means sign or trigger.

Lean Production   A term roughly synonymous with Just-in-Time/Total Quality Control.

Logistics   In an industrial context, this term refers to the functions of obtaining and distributing material and product.

Manufacturing Resource Planning (MRP II) A people-based technology for the effective planning of the resources of a manufacturing company. Ideally, it addresses operational planning in units, financial planning in dollars, and has a simulation capability to answer "what if" questions.

Master Production Schedule The anticipated build schedule, representing what the company plans to produce expressed in specific items, configurations, quantities and dates.

Material Requirements Planning (MRP) A set of techniques which uses bills of material, inventory data, and the master production schedule to calculate requirements for items.

Materials Management An organizational structure which groups all or most of the functions related to the complete cycle of material flow, from the purchase and internal control of production materials, to the planning and control of work-in-process, to the warehousing, shipping, and distribution of the finished product.

Mission Statement A formal statement of the organization's purpose, why it exists.

Mistake-Proofing Designing products and processes so that it's impossible to make them incorrectly. In Japanese, Poka-yoke.

MRP See: Material Requirements Planning.

MRP II See: Manufacturing Resource Planning.

Opportunity Evaluator A technique to help select improvement initiatives that support the customer-focused strategy.

Pareto's Law A concept developed by Vilfredo Pareto, an Italian economist, stating that a small percentage of a group accounts for the largest fraction of the impact, value, etc. Syn: Pareto analysis.

Pay for Knowledge See: Skill Based Pay.

People Empowerment The practice of giving non-managerial employees the responsibility and the power to make decisions regarding their jobs or tasks.

Plan-Do-Check-Action A bedrock technique within Total Quality Control, this refers to the process of a continuously rotating wheel of activities to solve quality problems. Also called the Deming Circle, after its developer.

Plant-Within-a-Plant The establishment of semi-autonomous manufacturing units within a larger plant.

Poka-Yoke   Japanese term for Mistake-Proofing.

Pull System   See: Kanban.

Push System   Refers to how material is moved on the plant floor. Push indicates that material moves to the next operation automatically upon completion of the prior operation.

QFD   Acronym for Quality Function Deployment.

Quality at the Source   Creating the capability and responsibility for 100 percent quality as part of the production process. Separate inspection steps can then normally be eliminated.

Quality Function Deployment (QFD)   A people-based technology for rigorously determining customer needs and desires, translating these into technical product requirements, and driving these requirements into specific design values for components, materials, and production processes.

Rough-Cut Capacity Planning   The process of converting the production plan and/or the master production schedule into the capacity needs for key resources: manpower, machinery, warehouse space, vendors' capabilities, and in some cases, money.

Sales and Operations Planning   The process of setting the overall levels of sales, production and other activities to meet the Business Plan, and tracking actual performance to those plans.

SBP   Acronym for Skill Based Pay.

Simultaneous Engineering   See: Design for Manufacturability.

Single Minute Exchange of Dies (SMED)   An approach to reduce setup and changeover times to less than ten minutes.

Skill Based Pay (SBP)   A compensation approach where people's pay is based not only on what job they're doing at a specific time, but also on how many different jobs they are qualified to do and how many different skills they have mastered.

SMED   Acronym for Single Minute Exchange of Dies.

SPC   Acronym for Statistical Process Control.

Statistical Process Control (SPC)   A set of techniques based on the continuous measurement of processes and/or products during production. The goal of SPC is to eliminate the productionof defects, by indicating in advance when a process is going out of control. SPC is a key element of Total Quality Control.

Strategic Planning   The process of developing and executing plans to reach a defined set of high-level goals. Strategies can exist at the corporate level, at the business unit level, and at the operational level within the business unit.

Synchronous Manufacturing The practice of finishing, fabricating, and procuring in synchronization, i.e. suppliers producing and providing just what's needed for fabrication, and fabricating just what's needed for finishing.

Total Quality Control (TQC) A people-based technology whose goal is the assurance of quality at the point where the work is performed. It includes the set of tools and techniques which enable people to solve problems and thereby improve quality—Statistical Process Control, Cause-and-Effect Diagrams, Pareto Diagramming, Root Cause Analysis, and many others.

Total Quality Management (TQM) Frequently used as an all-encompassing term, to cover all of operational excellence. As such, it addresses far more than conformance quality and/or product performance.

TQC Acronym for Total Quality Control.

TQE Acronym for Total Quality Excellence. See: Total Quality Management.

TQL Acronym for Total Quality Leadership. See: Total Quality Management.

TQM Acronym for Total Quality Management.

TQP Acronym for Total Quality Pursuit. See: Total Quality Management.

Trade-Off Matrix A technique used to prioritize the competitive elements in a business, so that impediments to providing high customer satisfaction can be eliminated.

Vision Statement A formal statement as to the direction of the organization, i.e., where is it going and what does it want to become.

Workload Estimator A technique to help prevent overloading the people implementing major improvement initiatives.

Notes

CHAPTER 1: IS YOUR COMPANY AT RISK?

1. Certainly there can be cases where an opportunity that doesn't fit the strategy is so compelling that it causes the strategy to be reviewed and perhaps modified. But these are few and far between, and they will be obvious.
2. PIMS uses the term "perceived quality." I prefer "customer satisfaction" because it is clearer and more widely understood.
3. *The PIMS Principles*, by Robert D. Buzzell and Bradley T. Gale (New York: The Free Press, 1987).

CHAPTER 2: STRATEGIC PLANNING—WHAT, WHY, WHERE, AND WHO

1. *Strategic Direction*, Fairfax, Vir., January 1988.
2. From *Webster's Seventh New Collegiate Dictionary* (Springfield, Mass.: G.&C. Merriam Company), 1969.
3. Michael Porter refers to this as the "competitive strategy." See *Competitive Strategy*, by Michael E. Porter (New York: The Free Press, 1980).
4. As quoted in *The Boeing News*, the weekly Boeing newspaper for its employees, on Jan. 25, 1991.
5. In English, in the order listed: Total Quality Control, Total Quality Management, Employee Involvement, Electronic Data Interchange, Just-in-Time, Flexible Manufacturing Systems, Automated Guided Vehicles, Material Requirements Planning, Manufacturing Resource Planning, Statistical Process Control, Skill Based Pay, Design for

Competitive Advantage, Quality Function Deployment, Activity Based Costing, trigger, warning light, continuous improvement, mistake-proofing.

CHAPTER 3: BREAKING THE RULES: ZERO TRADE-OFFS

1. For more details, see *On Patrol With Tellabs Batchbusters*, an Oliver Wight Executive Report, available from the Oliver Wight Companies, 85 Allen Martin Drive, Essex Junction, Vt. 05452.
2. A level of excellence, similar to an "A" grade in school. See Chapter 11, which addresses the ABCD Checklist.
3. It's now possible to implement most of Manufacturing Resource Planning on a low-cost, quick-payback, high-yield, and proven basis. The approach is called Quick Slice MRP and is spelled out in *MRP II: Making It Happen*, 2nd Ed., by Thomas F. Wallace (Essex Junction, Vt.: Oliver Wight Publications, 1990).
4. *Industry Week*, Aug. 6, 1990.

CHAPTER 4: CUSTOMERS—THE REASON FOR BEING

1. *Consumer Reports*, September 1990.
2. *The Marketing Edge*, by George E. Palmatier and Joseph S. Shull (Essex Junction, Vt.: Oliver Wight Publications, 1989).
3. Pareto's Law refers to the principle of the "vital few—trivial many." For example, in many companies 30 to 60 percent of their sales comes from 5 to 10 percent of their products. Pareto's Law is also used extensively within Just-in-Time and Total Quality Control, and forms the basis for ABC inventory analysis.
4. Andre Martin refers to this process of informational linking as "Customer Connectivity" and discusses it thoroughly in his book *DRP: Distribution Resource Planning* (Essex Junction, Vt.: Oliver Wight Publications, 1990).

CHAPTER 5: PEOPLE—THE HEART

1. See Grace Pastiak's "Web of Inclusion," *New York Times Business Section*, May 5, 1991.
2. *Fortune* (special edition), "The New American Century," 1991.

3. *Industry Week*, Feb. 3, 1992.
4. *The New York Times*, April 6, 1978.
5. *Financial World*, Sept. 3, 1991.
6. *Industry Week*, Dec. 3, 1990.
7. *Strategic Direction*, April 1990.
8. They taught me about TQC also back in the Sixties, using a text titled *Total Quality Control* by Armand V. Feigenbaum, New York, McGraw-Hill, 1961. It made a lot of sense to me, and I couldn't figure out why hardly anyone was doing it.
9. Also called Pay-for-Knowledge (PFK).
10. For more information, see "The People of Milliken," *Target* magazine, Fall 1990, from the Association for Manufacturing Excellence, Wheeling, Ill. 60090.

CHAPTER 6: NEW PRODUCTS—THE LIFEBLOOD

1. *The Customer Driven Company*, by William E. Eureka and Nancy E. Ryan (Dearborn, Mich.: ASI Press, 1988).
2. Ibid.
3. Ibid.
4. Ibid.
5. Ibid.

CHAPTER 7: CONTINUOUS IMPROVEMENT—THE CONSCIENCE

1. *Industry Week*, Nov. 5, 1990.
2. *Fortune*, Nov. 19, 1990.
3. *Automotive Week*, Nov. 15, 1990.
4. To get the full treatment, see *Just-in-Time: Making It Happen*, by William A. Sandras, Jr. (Essex Junction, Vt.: Oliver Wight Publications, 1989).
5. Ibid.
6. *Total Quality Control*, by Armand V. Feigenbaum (New York: McGraw-Hill, 1961).
7. Per *Quality Is Free*, by Phil Crosby (New York: McGraw-Hill, 1979).
8. *Quest for Quality*, by Hale, Hoelscher, and Kowal (Minneapolis, Minn.: The Tennant Company, 1987).
9. *Made in the USA*, by Hale, Hoelscher, Kowal, and Sehnert (Minneapolis, Minn.: The Tennant Company, 1991).

10. *Zero Quality Control: Source Inspection and the Poka-yoke System*, by Shigeo Shingo (Cambridge, Mass.: Productivity Press, 1986).
11. Courtesy of *Approach*, the U.S. Navy flight-safety magazine, from about thirty years ago when I was in that business.
12. Malcolm Baldrige National Quality Aware 1991 Application Guidelines, United States Department of Commerce, National Institute of Standards and Technology, Gaithersburg, Md. 20899.
13. As quoted in *Chief Executive*, September 1990.
14. "Being 'Baldrige-Eligible' Isn't Enough," by Jerry Bowles and Joshua Hammond, *The New York Times*, Sept. 22, 1991.

CHAPTER 8: TACTICAL PLANNING AND CONTROL— THE CENTRAL NERVOUS SYSTEM

1. The dispatching function is part of what's frequently called "Shop Floor Control," which consists also of work order generation, operation-by-operation reporting, and input/output tracking to ensure that each work center is producing at the volumes required by the capacity plan.
2. One of the reasons this misunderstanding is so widespread is because that's how it's been presented by many of the suppliers of MRP II software. They sell MRP II as a computer solution. The first-rate software suppliers, the really good ones, know better and present their product accordingly.
3. Spread-sheet software can be helpful in what-if analyses at the aggregate level, i.e., Sales and Operations Planning and related Rough-Cut Capacity Planning. For simulation at the more detailed levels (Master Scheduling and "below" in Figure 8-1), the full MRP II data base needs to be accessed, and this is beyond the scope of most spread-sheet packages.
4. *Climbing the Peaks of Success*, an Oliver Wight Executive Report, Essex Junction, Vt.

CHAPTER 9: FACILITIES AND EQUIPMENT— THE MUSCLE AND BONE, PART I

1. "The Focused Factory," by Wickham Skinner, *Harvard Business Review*, May–June 1974.
2. *Industry Week*, Nov. 5, 1990.

3. One could make a good case that this discussion of plant focus belongs more appropriately in the chapter on people. I won't argue with that. Howewver, I put it here because it fits so closely with our next topic: flow.

4. *Radio Cap Paints a New Future*, an Oliver Wight Executive Report, Essex Junction, Vt.

5. A job shop, per this definition, is a micro example of process focus.

6. *Just-in-Time*, by Walter E. Goddard (Essex Junction, Vt.: Oliver Wight Publications, 1966).

7. The next one I see will be the first one I've ever seen, and I've been involved with manufacturing for almost thirty years.

8. *21st Century Manufacturing: Becoming a World Class Performer*, by Thomas A. Gunn (New York: Harper Business, 1992).

CHAPTER 10: SUPPLY CHAIN—THE MUSCLE AND BONE, PART II

1. *Business Week*, March 3, 1986.

2. For an example of one company's migration from conventional purchasing (requisitions and hard-copy purchase orders) to EDI, see "Faxban: Kanban Meets the Fax Machine," *Target* magazine, Fall 1990. The word *faxban* refers to the company's use of transmitting kanban triggers to their suppliers via the fax machine. It worked superbly, but after a while the increased volume made that process unwieldy and they migrated to EDI.

3. *Business Week*, Feb. 17, 1992.

4. *Distribution Resource Planning*, 2nd Ed., by Andre J. Martin (Essex Junction, Vt.: Oliver Wight Publications, 1990).

CHAPTER 11: MEASUREMENTS—THE VITAL SIGNS

1. This refers to a defect rate of fewer than four pieces per million. It is effectively, although perhaps not literally, zero defects.

2. *The Oliver Wight ABCD Checklist for Operational Excellence* (Essex Junction, Vt.: Oliver Wight Publications, 1992).

3. *The Complete Guide to Activity Based Costing*, by Michael C. Gunn (New York: Prentice-Hall Press, 1991).

4. For an excellent treatment of ABC, see "Activity Based Costing: A Tool

for Manufacturing Excellence," by Peter B.B. Turney, *Target* magazine (Wheeling, Ill.), Summer 1989.

5. Some years ago we saw the same thing develop with MRP and the bills of material: only one company-wide bill of material inside the computer, but with flexible display capabilities for Engineering, Manufacturing, and Cost Accounting, so each group can see everything it needs to see, but no more.

6. "One Cost System Isn't Enough," by Robert S. Kaplan, *Harvard Business Review*, January–February 1988.

7. "How Hewlett-Packard Gets Numbers It Can Trust," Debbie Berlant, Reese Browning, and George Foster, *Harvard Business Review*, January–February 1990.

CHAPTER 12: CUSTOMER-DRIVEN STRATEGY—THE BRAIN

1. *Chief Executive*, September 1990.

APPENDIX A: MARKETPLACE AND FINANCIAL ASPECTS OF REDUCING SETUPS AND CHANGEOVERS

1. *A Revolution in Manufacturing: The SMED System*, by Shigeo Shingo (Cambridge, Mass.: Productivity Press, 1985).

Index